U. S. Military Patches of WWII

By *Christopher P. Brown*

TURNER PUBLISHING COMPANY
Paducah, Kentucky

TURNER PUBLISHING COMPANY
Publishers of America's History
412 Broadway • P.O. Box 3101
Paducah, KY 42002-3101
270-443-0121

By: Christopher P. Brown

Publishing Consultant: Douglas W. Sikes
Book Designer: Elizabeth B. Sikes
Cover Design: Emily K. Sikes

Library of Congress Control No.: 2002110258
ISBN:1-56311-830-0
Printed in the United States of America

LIMITED EDITION
Additional copies may be purchased from Turner Publishing Company.

CONTENTS

4

INTRODUCTION

This book was created for collectors of American WWII shoulder sleeve insignia. The information represents a thirty-year accumulation of facts extracted from countless books, research, experience, acquisitions, other experts, and hundreds of conversations with veterans. Inside you will find a wealth of information including:

Color photographs of hundreds of WWII shoulder sleeve insignia including common, scarce, and very rare designs. Unlike the vast majority of patch references, the patches pictured are authentic, period pieces. A few reproductions are used for comparison purposes and for reinforcing the methods of identifying reproductions.

Brief histories explaining the purpose and significant service locations of the units who wore these insignia during WWII.

Photographs and descriptions of the variations of each patch, which the collector may encounter. Like coins and stamps, variations or errors in design can have an incredible influence on the worth of a patch. Knowledge of these variations is absolutely essential and will pay enormous dividends.

Value assessments of the common, authorized designs as well as the values of the variations and unusual specimens.

Methods of determining authenticity which will assist in insuring that the collector acquires genuine specimens.

An explanation of definitions, abbreviations and terms used by collectors and dealers. Most books, catalogues, auction publications, and dealer lists include codes denoting type of manufacture, condition and other relevant information. A knowledge of these terms allows the collector to determine the period, authenticity, value, availability, and sometimes the origin of a particular piece.

Enlisted cloth rank insignia. Including the Army, Navy, Marine Corps, Army Air Force and Coast Guard. This section also discusses service stripes and other designators.

A list of Divisional nicknames. Unofficial "tabs" were produced, which bear the nickname or motto of a particular division. They were made for wear above or below the division patch. Over the years, these tabs frequently become separated and are often found for sale with no identifying information. This section will assist the collector in associating separated tabs with their correct patch.

Methods of wear. In some cases patches were worn on areas of the uniform other than the shoulder. Recognizing an improperly affixed patch may tip the collector that a uniform was pieced together and is not a genuine ensemble. On the other hand, some strange patch configurations were little-known exceptions to the rule and are quite correct, and often, quite valuable. This book provides information on method of wear for period insignia.

Internet auction survival tips. There is no greater resource available to collectors than the internet. However, the risk to unwary collectors is proportionately extreme. This section will help to provide you with some fundamental tips on negotiating the internet auctions.

As a beginning collector, I was repeatedly duped by unscrupulous dealers who convinced me to sell or trade an unidentified item, only to find out later that the item was extremely rare and valuable. Over the years, I have overpaid for common items represented as scarce, or reproductions represented as authentic pieces. I have passed on items at yard sales, offered for a dollar, but negotiable, and discovered later the item was worth hundreds. I have paid hundreds and discovered the item was worth nothing. Collectors miss incredible opportunities every day. Just as frequently, collectors make dreadfully expensive mistakes. Through obsessive study and exhaustive research, I have managed to negotiate the learning curve and emerge with some degree of wisdom and expertise on this subject.

The endeavor here is to assist beginning and veteran enthusiasts in assembling collections of authentic, period insignia without the heartbreak, expense, and frustration suffered through lack of knowledge. It is to offer decades of education and experience to the reader in permanent, accessible, written form. And, most importantly, it is the self satisfaction of helping those that share my passion.

The value of any collectible item is subjective at best. Prices are affected by region, provenance, local collector competition, and individual desire to possess a particular piece. As a result of the internet, price lists that were accurate one year ago, are completely inaccurate today. The values listed in this book are based upon prolonged involvement with the subject, constant analysis of internet auctions, traditional auction house results, gun shows, military shows, flea markets and well established mail order lists and publications. These values represent competitive retail prices. With patience, patches can always be found at substantially lower prices. Although this book concentrates on WWII vintage patches, I have included examples of current and reproduction patches to help illustrate the disparity in value between vintage WWII, and reproduction/current items.

Most collecting guides provide one representative example of a particular patch, which does not reflect the value of common and rare variations. To a beginning collector a black and white photograph or drawing of an 8th Army Air Force patch appears the same whether it is of intricate bullion construction or factory embroidered. The value however, may vary by $50.00 or more. Patches are Like coins and stamps. A slight variation in color, detail, shape, or intentional or unintentional alteration can cause an enormous difference in worth. In this book, you will see clear and unmistakable examples of many variations and will understand how to associate a realistic value with a particular type or construction of insignia. Special attention has been paid to the photographs to insure that the collector understands and can identify, even the subtle differences in design. And also, to some extent, the area of manufacture to include insignia made in America, Australia, England, Italy, Germany, or China, Burma, and India.

Probably of greatest value to the collector, this book provides simple methods of determining the likely authenticity of period items with merely a glance. After reviewing this section even a beginning collector will know precisely what to look for that will identify a patch as being authentic or reproduction, old or new. After some review, the "repros" will be instantly obvious.

NOTE: Aside from fully embroidered types, most American shoulder sleeve insignia designs from WWII can be frequently found in several varieties including: felt on felt, embroidered on felt, bullion, and embroidered on twill. Additionally, almost every design can be found with or without an olive drab (green) border. Some of these variants are much scarcer than others. I wanted to establish this at the beginning of the book so that reader will consider it common knowledge that nearly every patch exists in at least those varieties. The disparity in values between these types will be better understood after viewing representative examples of each throughout the book. Aside from these five variation types, the author has illustrated or described many known variations as well as interesting characteristics associated with the patches illustrated. There are so many minor variations of each patch design that it would be impossible to list and illustrate them all. For instance, the Eighth Army Air Force and China Burma India patches both exist in thousands of variations if the smallest details are considered. For the purposes of this book, the author has defined "variation" as a significant deviation from the design generally accepted as the norm, or as officially approved by military authority. Major alterations in material, detail, shape, color, and size are considered significant.

PREFACE

Who knows why something strikes the fancy of a child. Whether it's the colors or the feel. Perhaps it represents something associated with a warm memory. Or maybe it somehow triggers a magical connection to the romantic, imaginative world that only a child can breath life to. I think it was the latter for me. When I opened the cedar chest in my grandparent's spare room, I was enveloped by the distinctive aroma of moth balls and cedar, which instantly extinguished any consciousness of the present. It was the aroma that I will ever-after associate with history.

Inside the chest was a collection of mysterious things; ominous things; in a little boy's mind, maybe even frightening and dangerous things. I vividly remember debating on whether these were things to be touched, or just looked at. I remember thinking that perhaps by my viewing them, it was already too late for me. Steeling myself, in preparation for whatever the consequences might be, I reached into the chest and touched them.

First, a large, heavy metal buckle. It was gray and evenly covered with a dark patina. It just looked evil. There was a raised crown and mysterious writing "GOTT MIT UNS". I had seen the bad guys wearing the same sort of thing every Saturday, on my favorite series Combat. I was taken by its weight and dark, sinister appearance. There was another heavy, oversized buckle with an elaborately stylized eagle on it. I clearly remember being sobered by the fact that these were real. Even a boy of eight, like me, knew that something dreadful had happened to the human beings that had worn these things before my Grandfather salvaged them as souvenirs.

I had now handled relics of war. I had touched things that were once owned by fallen soldiers. Not plastic men that could be righted again for the next battle, but real soldiers. I remember being happy that a little boy wasn't pulling my Grandfather's buckle out of a cedar chest in Germany. I remember feeling sad for the little boy in Germany that didn't have a cedar chest to go through because he didn't have a Grandfather.

The next items were a pair of shoulder boards. Thick, gray wool rectangles with a white piping all around the edges, and "412", in twisted red chord, embroidered across each. Eventually I came to a green, prickly wool tunic. On one shoulder was a bright red felt half-circle with a silver bullion lightning bolt running diagonally from one side to the other. The patch of the 78th Infantry Division. Below

this were the chevrons of a sergeant, with a small diamond underneath. Small discs of chocolate colored metal adorned each side of the rigid collar. One had crossed cannons in the middle, with "307" above and "C" below. The other disc had simply "US". On the breast was a rainbow colored ribbon with four tiny metal stars. Beneath this was a book entitled "History of the 307th Artillery regiment, Company C, 1917-1918. Another book had the red half-circle and lightning bolt design on the cover, along with "History of the 78th Division, 1917-1918". Piles of photographs, an age-yellowed map of some mysterious foreign place called the "Foret D'Argonne", a stack of letters secured with a bowed ribbon, and many other things. I had smelled history for the first time. I had touched history for the first time. I was hooked on history, forever.

Armed with these items and a fascination for military history, I began collecting and learning about the subject as best I could with very limited resources. Five dollars would still buy a handful of patches at a gun show. Neighbors and friends of the family gladly handed over souvenirs they had brought home, when I went on door to door collecting expeditions.

As the years have gone by my collection has taken on a new meaning for me. I have interviewed countless veterans and read hundreds of books. As a police officer, I have experienced gunfights. I have lost a sister and many friends to line of duty accidents or violence. Each event, each loss, is cumulative. Each one adds its own emotional and physical burden. But in terms of volume, they pale in comparison to the experiences of thousands of men and women who served and suffered in combat. I now have the maturity to understand what these patches represent. What, in the beginning, had no meaning to me other than their historic and visual interest, now symbolize collections of emotions and experiences that defy articulation. War requires people, with no malice for anyone and living ordinary and organized lives, to exchange this normalcy for unimaginable chaos and suffering. Political, moral, intellectual, and religious opinions do not deflect bullets, do not silence the thunder of an artillery barrage, do not warm a frozen body, and do not quell the uncertainties of life and death. An individual's sense of right and wrong, emotional and physical fortitude, and the unwavering allegiance to one's buddies are the primary factors in a soldier's ability to perform under sustained violence on the sea, in the air, or on the field. I cannot verbalize my admiration for those who have died, been wounded, or have otherwise been forever impacted by their military duties. Not because they wanted to be, but because they considered themselves to be an acceptable price to pay for their nation, their family, their friends, and their visions. I can think of no finer tribute to these people than to salvage and display the symbols of their sacrifice.

The collecting of military artifacts is nothing new. It has however, in the last several years exploded into one of the nation's fastest growing hobbies. This has had a significant impact on the collecting market for a number of reasons. As the demand for military antiques has increased greatly, so has the number of pieces hoarded in private collections. With so many items out of circulation, prices have skyrocketed accordingly. Many items increasing in value by several hundred percent. Even the most common items are progressively becoming more difficult to find. Many patches considered to be fairly common twenty years ago are either impossible to locate, or are so expensive now, that the average collector simply cannot afford to buy them.

As of the writing of this book, some one thousand WWII veterans are passing away each day. As the Second World War fades further and further into history, what used to be a continuous flow of items found at moving sales, garage sales, and estate sales has slowed to little more than a trickle. As the supply has diminished, the demand has increased. Thus, enters the counterfeiter.

The military collectible market has been thoroughly flooded with reproductions of everything from the most common, to the rarest patches. Over the years, the quality of reproductions has improved as well. Any military show, gun show, or flea market will reveal an abundance of reproduced material manufactured for the purpose of deceiving the unsuspecting collector. Without close inspection and some knowledge, reproductions are often impossible to identify. When dealers are confronted with the questionable provenance of such pieces, the predictable response is denial or ignorance. Some will state indignantly "you don't see *original* marked anywhere do you"? But, when a reproduction is priced comparably to a vintage piece, the price tag implies that is offered as an original.

Reputable dealers will clearly identify reproductions, (also referred to frequently as "collector copies), and will offer them for a couple dollars; their maximum worth. They are offered as representative fillers until an original can be found. Unfortunately however, too many military show, flea market, internet, and gun show dealers neglect to make the distinction to prospective buyers. Usually in fact, they are aggressively marketed as genuine.

So, is it impossible to find World War II insignia these days? Absolutely not. Is it impossible to tell the difference between genuine pieces and the fakes? Absolutely not. Do you need enormous sums of money to assemble a great collection of vintage insignia? No. You simply need to know where to look, how to tell the good from the bad, and what is a fair price to pay. With a trained eye and some perseverance, the collector will be amazed at how often a genuine treasure can be found at a nominal price. With an understanding of the material in this book, a little patience, and a few dollars, you will be on your way to a successful and gratifying collection.

 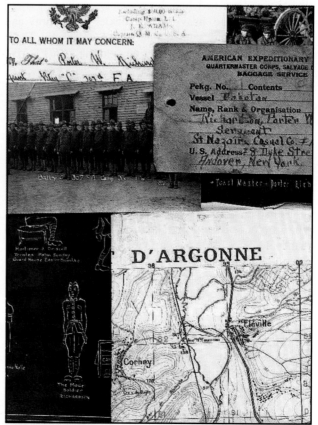

Items from the cedar chest. The precursors for a lifetime fascination.

This book is dedicated to:
Lisa G. Wampole
Who believed in me, despite me.
&
Regina Brown, Porter Richardson, and John Richardson.
You are my heroes.

My sister, Lisa G. Wampole

My mother Regina, US Coast Guard, Elizabeth City,
North Carolina, 1944.

My Grandfather, Porter Richardson
307th Field Artillery, 78th Division, 1918.

My Uncle, John Richardson,
Army Service Forces / ETO Comm. Zone, 1944

ARMY GROUPS

The Army Groups were a result of the incredible scope of WWII and are unique to that conflict. Army Groups coordinated the strategic activities of multiple armies. Like army and corps staffs, these units assumed administrative responsibilities including logistics and planning, thus allowing subordinate staffs to concentrate on actual combat activities.

1st Army Group

Left: Standard type - $12.00. **Right:** Rare variation with red "I" - $75.00. It is uncertain if the red variation was an error or if it was deliberately produced. It has been theorized that this patch was unofficially worn by 1st Army Group artillery components. *Service:* Among other things, the First Army Group was responsible for planning the invasion of Europe (D-Day). In 1944, it was redesignated as the Twelfth Army Group. Some activities were continued in England using the First Army Group title. These activities were part of Operation Fortitude and were intended to give the Germans the impression that an entire army group was staging in England and poised for attack. The objective was to convince the Germans that Normandy was merely a diversion and that the actual invasions would occur in Norway, and the Pas-de-Calais area.

6th Army Group variations

Standard types with factory variations in the design - $8.00 each. **Left:** Note that there are interruptions in the thatch design and the overall patch has a coarser weave. **Right:** This patch has solid a white thatch design with no interruptions. *Service:* This group was assembled initially to orchestrate the invasion of Southern France. It played a major role in the Battle of the Bulge, fought its way to the allied forces in Italy, and later entered Austria.

First Army Group, red variation in reverse with original vendor tag still affixed

12th Army Group

Standard type - $8.00. This patch can be found with a dark army green border. The army green leads some collectors to believe that the patch is post-1957, when army green was adopted. But the 12th is one of the rare examples of army green border being applied to a WWII patch. *Service:* Formed in July 1944, to coordinate the efforts of several American armies. It participated in combat on the Brittany Peninsula, Siegfried Line, and the Ruhr. Some portions of the group entered Austria. It was the largest command in American military history.

15th Army Group variations

Standard types - $12.00. **Left:** Embroidered on a khaki base fabric. **Right:** Embroidered on an olive drab base fabric. Khaki and olive drab are the most common base fabric colors used in WWII patch construction. Machines would simply sew rows of patch designs onto strips of fabric. Only a couple of inches separated one patch from the next. The fabric strips would then be cut into individual squares, with one patch in the middle of each square. To finish the patches, the excess fabric was trimmed from around the patch. The only trace left of the base fabric is visible by looking at the extreme edge of the patch. This manufacturing style resulted in the term "cut-edge" patch, which is indicative of 1940s-1950s manufacture. *Service:* This group was organized as a joint British/American command. Organized in North Africa, it conducted the invasion of Sicily and Italy. The group was inactivated after Italy capitulated.

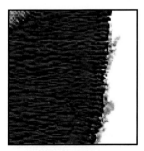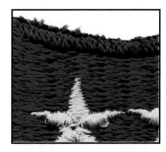

The factory manufacturing process for fully embroidered WWII patches resulted in the "cut-edge" appearance. The edges are normally khaki or olive drab, but may be other colors as well.

Patch Manufacturing Process

Step 1: Row of patch designs sewn onto base fabric. (Base fabric in this example is olive drab, but may be khaki or other colors).

Step 2: The strip of fabric is then cut into individual squares, with one patch per square.

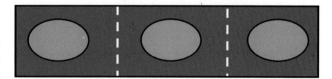

Step 3: Excess base fabric is then cut from around edge of patch.

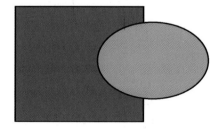

Step 4: Finished patch with just a trace of the base fabric remaining at extreme edges.

ARMIES

There was no uniformly prescribed composition for the armies during WWII. They varied greatly and remained in a constant state of flux. Armies were assembled based on the strategic and tactical requirements of the moment. Their purpose was to direct and orchestrate the operations of multiple corps and their respective conglomerations of assigned units. These organizations had some organic components, but specialized groups would be attached and detached as the situation dictated.

THEATER OF OPERATION:

European Theater of Operations (ETO) for the purposes of this book, the ETO includes Africa and the Mediterranean. 1st, 3rd, 5th, 7th, 9th and 15th Armies.

Pacific Theater of Operations, 6th, 8th and 10th Armies.

American Theater of Operations, 2nd and 4th Armies.

Fourteenth Army (Phantom), Operation Fortitude. This army actually existed only in the form of wireless traffic, documents, conversations, some patches, and an elaborate facade of pretend war material. This was part of the pre-D-Day deception program. It was designed to deceive German forces as to actual allied strength and the actual invasion location. Fourteenth Army patches were manufactured during WWII, although the army was nothing more than smoke and mirrors.

The First Army design is interesting because it was originally done in subdued colors (WWI and WWII), was later changed to full color (1950s-1960s), and has since returned to subdued on the battle dress uniform. The First Army patches with color inserts shown in the following photo are a continuation of a characteristic of many earlier designs. During WWI, it was common practice to identify specific components within an army or division by inserting branch of service colors or a symbol somewhere on the patch. Although discouraged by regulations later, these variations were still manufactured and worn.

All army patch designs, except the Seventh Army, incorporate the colors red and white. These are the flag colors that distinguish a field army. The Seventh Army colors (blue, red and yellow) denote the three major branches, infantry, artillery and cavalry. Excluding variations, there are 14 WW II Army patch designs.

1st Allied Airborne Army variations

Left: Standard English-made, machine embroidered on felt - $45.00+. **Right:** English-made, hand embroidered on felt type - $175.00. The hand-embroidered variation is quite rare. Note the omission of the word "ALLIED" and that the black section is a separate piece, which extends full width across the patch. This patch has an interesting provenance. The source, an American infantryman, found this patch in the pocket of a German soldier who, presumably, liberated it from an American prisoner or casualty. For a standard embroidered type - $20.00. *Service:* France, Holland, Germany and occupation duty. This was a combined allied army consisting of British and American airborne forces.

First Army patch. This is obvious because of the dark, army green border which was not introduced until 1957, and the merrowed edge which was not widely introduced until 1968 - $3.00.

The German soldier pictured above was killed in action in Thionville, France. It was during the search of a casualty like this one, that the pictured Allied Airborne patch was discovered.

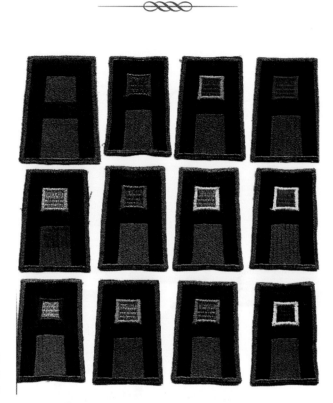

First Army variations with color inserts.

Top row - left to right: Standard 1st Army early design, Headquarters Personnel, Ordinance, and Artillery. **Middle row - left to right:** Infantry, Infantry (darker blue variation), Signal Corps, Engineers. **Bottom row - left to right:** Military Police, Cavalry, Quartermaster, Medical. The First Army color variations manufactured during WWII are somewhat scarce. They make a very attractive display and provide a sense of completeness to a cloth insignia collection. The collector should be cautioned that many reproduction designs are well made and come complete with vertical weave patterns and cotton threads. Collectors can expect to pay at least $35.00 for original color insert types. Rarer examples such as aviation, armor and finance will be substantially higher. Another variation features a gold "A". I am uncertain what the gold variation represents. For a standard fully embroidered First Army patch black and green - $3.00. *Service:* France, Belgium, Germany, (H.Q. staff spent time in the Philippines as well).

Variations of the First Army patch with the color insert include, but are not limited to: **Armored Force**, green and white __/ **Chemical Warfare**, cobalt blue and golden yellow __/ **Finance**, silver gray and golden yellow __/ **Medical**, maroon and white__/ **Military Police**, yellow and green__/ __/ **Quartermaster Corps**, buff__/ **Signal Corps**,

First Army later designs for comparison

Left: The full color cut-edge type is often times represented as WWII vintage, but the full color design was not adopted until after the war - $3.00. **Right:** A current issue

orange and white__/ **Tank Destroyer Forces**, orange and black__/ **Ordinance**, crimson and yellow__/ **Detached Enlisted Men**, grass green__/ **Aviation**, blue and orange__/ **Aviation variation** orange and blue __/ **Engineers**, red and white __/ **West Point**, white and yellow __/

* Note: In these descriptions the primary insert color is listed first and the trim color second..

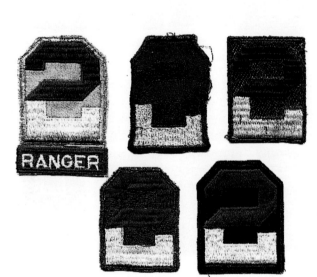

Second Army variations

Top row- Left: On khaki twill, with accompanying Ranger tab*. This tab is an unofficial type that is occasionally seen in use from 1942-1945. This khaki twill variant is harder to find - $10.00. **Middle:** Standard type with an unusually loose pattern to the weave - $4.00. **Right:** German-made, embroidered on a very coarse material. Note the square shape without angled corners. This shape is scarcer than the normal, angled corner type - $8.00. **Bottom row – Left:** Standard type - $3.00. **Right:** Standard current issue type. Note the dark army green background which means post-1957, and the merrowed edge which means post-1968 - $1.00. For an original RANGER tab like the one shown above - $40.00. *Service:* Primarily tasked with training duties in the United States. Several WWII patches can be found on khaki material and were in-

tended for wear on the summer khaki uniform.

* There is some confusion as to the origin and use of this Ranger tab. Much like today, there are soldiers assigned to Ranger units, and there are soldiers who are Ranger *qualified*, but are assigned to regular units. During WWII, the Ranger Battalions wore the Ranger diamond patch or the black scrolls. However many soldiers in regular units received certificates of proficiency after graduating from a Ranger course. These soldiers were sometimes allowed to wear the red and white Ranger tab in addition to their regular unit patch. The Ranger course topics included, but were not limited to: hand to hand combat, camouflage, a "blitz" course, booby traps and demolition, sniper techniques, infiltration, ambushes, improvised bridge building and toggle rope techniques. Many units, like the 104th Infantry Division, awarded attractive certificates to members completing the Ranger course.

Third Army patch variations

Left: An early, high quality example with a vertically ribbed appearance to the weave and an olive drab border - $8.00. **Right:** Standard embroidered type - $2.00. This patch can be found with some variation in the "A". I have seen one example that is fully embroidered in subdued colors with a distinctive insignia featuring a dragon embroidered between the legs of the "A". This patch appeared to be 1920s-1930s period and is a very unusual variation - $125.00. *Service:* France, Brittany, Belgium, Germany and Czechoslovakia.

Fourth Army embroidered variations

Four examples of Fourth Army embroidered variations. Note the different patterns in weave, and the differences in the stem thickness on the clover. ***Top left:*** This example has an olive drab border - $12.00. For any other embroidered type, despite minor variations - $4.00. *Service:* Primarily tasked with training duties in the United States.

described as "bevo", but this is not a bevo patch - $12.00. Comparatively few American patches were produced in a *true* bevo during WWII. Most were produced during the occupation period. A huge percentage of WWII German insignia were executed in a bevo weave. (See "Bevo" in the *"Terms and Abbreviations"* section for more information). ***Top right:*** Standard type - $3.00. ***Bottom:*** Silver bullion on felt, theater-made example. Many Fifth Army bullion types were made for members of the 509th Parachute Infantry, who were briefly attached to Fifth Army headquarters. There is a tab associated with the 509th that was worn over the Fifth Army patch, which is blue (sometimes with red trim) and "PARACHUTE" in white letters. These tabs are extremely rare. For a bullion Fifth Army patch - $50.00. For the 509th "PARACHUTE" tab - $400.00 +. It is apparent that the bullion example has been removed from a uniform. Signs of use such as the waves created by thread binding into the felt add some corroboration to authenticity. Although this particular characteristic can be faked, it is one indicator, which, when combined with other characteristics, can help you determine authenticity with some degree of confidence. Let's use this particular patch as an example. A collector examining this piece should note: 1) Quality bullion thread. 2) Dark, even patina on the bullion. 3) Aged appearance of the felt. 4) Signs of removal from a uniform. 5) A construction type consistent with the area where the unit served. 6) The hand-made and imperfect appearance of the reverse side. When considered collectively, there is no doubt that this is an original piece.

Fifth Army variations.

Three variations and construction styles of the 2nd design, Fifth Army patch. ***Top left:*** Theater made (Italian) example of woven, stiff material. This style is often

Fifth Army variations in reverse

This shows how a theater-made patch will typically appear on the reverse side. Sometimes the reverse is covered with fabric of some sort. *Service:* Morocco, Italy.

Fifth Army, 1st style

Embroidered on white felt octagon. This is a poor quality reproduction. The felt is brand new and stiff. The edges are clean and crisp. There are no signs of age or soiling. But the easiest method of identifying this as a fake is the ultraviolet (UV) light test. The patch reacts brilliantly under UV light. This patch was purchased on the Internet. The winning bid was $16.00 plus shipping and insurance (another $3.50). The patch was represented as 100% original, but there was no photograph available from the vendor. My recommendation, based on personal experience with the internet is, if you can't see it, both front and back, don't pursue it. For an original - $15.00.

Fully embroidered Fifth Army, 1st style
Fully embroidered type - $45.00.

Sixth Army embroidered variations
Top left: Khaki standard type - $5.00. **Top right:** Coarse weave, fully embroidered type, in a medium green. Most

likely German-made and dating from the Occupation period - $5.00. **Bottom:** 1957 or later example. Note how the background color has changed to army green to match the new army green uniform. This is a transitional piece. The color has been changed, but it retains the cut-edge rather than a merrowed edge - $2.00. This second style Sixth Army patch replaced the first style design in 1945. *Service:* New Britain, Admiralty Islands, New Guinea, Philippines. The Sixth also performed occupation duty in Japan.

Sixth Army, 1st style

Fully embroidered example of the 1st style patch, worn from 1927-1945 - $12.00. Pre-WWII versions were embroidered of felt.

Seventh Army, German-made variations

Top: German, machine embroidered type. The texture is very different than U.S. machine-made patches. The tab is also German-made. **Bottom:** Is a German bevo-like example - $7.00. *Service:* Italy, Southern France, and Germany.

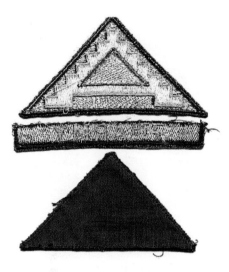

Seventh army, German-made variations in reverse
Note the distinctive thread patterns on the back of the top patch and tab. The bottom patch has a black fabric backing applied. Applied backing is common. The variations in backing material and color are endless.

Showing the reverse side of the Seventh Army TTC patch.
A German machine-embroidered patch produced during the period of occupation. The patch and tab are one piece (integral). An original TTC patch is very difficult to find - $165.00.

Bullion Seventh Army patch and tab
A German bullion example in gold metal threads on felt. The accompanying tab is another commonly encountered accessory for the 7th Army patch: "SEVEN STEPS TO HELL". For this patch and tab $45.00.

Eighth Army patches
Left: WWII standard type. Note the khaki base material visible around the edge - $2.00. **Right:** Current type. The merrowed edge is immediately obvious with its high border and the chain stitch running around the inside edge of the border. At the bottom left corner you can see the frayed remnants where the pigtail was cut off - $1.00. *Service:* New Guinea, New Britain, Philippines, numerous island engagements, Okinawa and occupation duty in Japan. After its Pacific service during WWII, the Eighth Army began its extended association with Korea. Consequently, myriad Eighth Army patches are found in foreign-made configurations including machine and hand-embroidered designs. Many are adorned with bullion, sequins and tinsels. Various tabs, both attached and separate, also exist. A few originated from the Philippines and other Pacific locations during WWII, but the vast majority are from the Korean War or later. Often times these later variations will be offered as WWII vintage. This information is offered for purely technical purposes. Despite being a few years younger than WWII patches, the

German-made (occupation period) Seventh Army Tank Training Center patch

Korean variations command prices similar to their WWII counterparts. They are equally attractive, the craftsmanship is excellent, and collectors find them just as desirable.

Fourteenth Army (Phantom)

Standard type - $20.00. **Fourteenth Army service:** See the comments at the beginning of the "ARMIES" section for details. *Service:* Ghost/phantom unit, Operation Fortitude.

Ninth Army

Standard type - $5.00. *Service:* France, Belgium, Luxembourg, The Netherlands, Germany, and occupation duty in Germany.

Tenth Army

Collectors have boundless latitude in defining what constitutes a "variation" for the purposes of their respective collections. Can you detect the difference in these two U.S. embroidered types? ***Left:*** Has the white triangles applied over the red. ***Right:*** Has the red applied over the white. For standard Tenth Army types like these - $5.00. *Service:* The Tenth Army was composed of Army and Marine units. It served in the Ryukyus Islands and Okinawa**.**

Fifteenth Army

Standard type - $8.00. Service: France, Germany and occupation duties in Germany.

ARMY CORPS

The Army Corps of the 1940's was responsible for orchestrating the activities of multiple divisions and attached support units including, but not limited to, engineers, cavalry, artillery, signals and tank destroyers. In practice however, like the armies, corps remained flexible in a structural and organizational sense. The tactical situation often dictated the corps composition. Although any operations typically required an infantry and armor combination, other units were attached or detached as needed. In all, 36 WWII era corps patches exist excluding the multitude of variations. Most corps patch designs incorporate the colors blue and white. These are the distinguishing flag colors of a field corps. The seven exceptions to this color scheme are the 1st, 9th, 12th, 13th, 14th, 19th (first design), and the 20th Corps. The armored corps patches utilize the standard armor triangle design and color scheme. armored corps are numbered with Roman numerals.

THEATER OF OPERATION:

European Theater of Operation (For the purposes of this book, includes Africa and the Mediterranean)**:** 2nd, 3rd, 4th, 5th, 6th, 7th, 8th, 12th, 13th, 15th, 16th, 18th- Airborne, 19th, 20th, 21st, 22nd, 23rd, 1st-Armored,

Pacific Theater of Operation: 1st, 9th, 10th, 11th, 14th, 24th,

American Theater of Operation: 36th.

Thirty-first and **Thirty-fourth Corps, (ghost / phantom units)**. There is confusion regarding the terms "phantom" or "ghost" units. Some units were slated for activation but due to costs and other factors, were never organized. Other units were developed on paper as part of Operation Fortitude. This operation involved deceiving Axis commanders as to the strength and location of the imminent cross-channel invasion (D-Day). Axis intelligence went so far as to plant and recruit employees in insignia manufacturing businesses. New patch designs represented new units being organized. By monitoring the new patch designs being manufactured, agents were able to assist the Axis intelligence branch in calculating American strength. Prior to D-Day, fourteen infantry divisions, five airborne divisions, two corps, and one army design were ordered and produced in limited quantities. Other details describing the organization and structure of these new units were "leaked" to various sources as well. This, combined with a number of other elaborate schemes gave the Germans a very exaggerated estimate of the available allied forces preparing for invasion. These latter designs that were manufactured as part of the deception strategy are the ghost or phantom units. These patches represent a very important aspect of WWII cloth insignia. They are necessary components of a complete collection. The Thirty-first and Thirty-fourth Corps are ghost/phantoms.

First Armored Corps (Not available for illustration) was originally part of the Task Force that assaulted Casablanca, Media, and French Morocco. Shortly thereafter, it assumed the title of I Armored Corps. The corps also participated in the invasion of Sicily, but was re-designated as the Seventh Army. **Second Armored, Third Armored** and **Fourth Armored Corps.** These units were re-designated prior to combat service. The Second Armored became part of the Eighteenth Corps, The Third Armored became the Nineteenth Corps, and the Fourth Armored became the Twentieth Corps. The **Eighteenth Armored Corps** patch is believed to have been used after the Second Armored Corps was re-designated as the Eighteenth Corps, and prior to the Eighteenth Corps adopting the dragon head design - $400.00+. A **Fifth Armored Corps** patch was produced during the war, but the unit was never activated - $200.00.

II Armored Corps

V Armored Corps (very scarce)

III Armored Corps

XVIII Armored Corps (ultra rare)

The XVIII Armored Corps patch was unofficially adopted in October, 1943 when the II Armored Corps was re-designated. Some factory embroidered examples exist, but many patches were improvised by adding the "XVIII" to the Armored Force patch by hand or on a home sewing machine. In February 1945, the XVIII Corps adopted the dragon head patch and the armored style patch was discontinued. Due to the value of an original patch, and because many of the originals were hand-made this patch is easily and frequently reproduced. Collectors interested in an original should seek a factory-embroidered type. Examine the back of the patch closely. Originals will have "snow" on the reverse. Snow should be visible on the back of the Roman numerals and should appear consistent with the snow elsewhere on the reverse. An absence of snow on the numerals or a different color or pattern of snow on the numerals indicates that they were added after the patch was manufactured. Most importantly, the lightning bolt should be sewn *over* the last one or two numerals. That aspect of the patch

IV Armored Corps

cannot be easily reproduced. The example shown here had the Roman numerals applied to an existing patch. Although snow appears on the back of the numerals and lightning bolt, I am doubtful of its authenticity.

low (cavalry) - $75.00. *Service:* Algeria, Morocco, Tunisia, Sicily, Italy, served on occupation duty in Austria and Italy.

1st Army Corps
Referred to as "I" Corps due to the similarity between the Roman numeral for one, and the letter "I", and because of the patch's resemblance to an eye. Standard type - $5.00. *Service:* East Indies, Papua, New Guinea, Philippines, served occupation duty in Japan.

3rd Army Corps
Standard type - $3.00. This particular patch can be found as frequently with an olive drab border as without. *Service:* France, Belgium, Germany.

2nd Army Corps
Standard type - $5.00. Variations can be found with a colored backing representing branch of service. These include: green (recon), red (artillery) and yel-

4th Army Corps
Standard type - $6.00. *Service:* Italy.

5th Army Corps variations
Left: German-made variation with red border. This design was worn unofficially by members of the 5th Corps artillery - $15.00. **Right:** Standard type - $4.00. *Service:* France, Germany, Czechoslovakia.

7th Army Corps (2nd style)
Standard type - $5.00. In 1958, when the army green uniform was adopted, the background color of this patch changed from olive drab (like this one) to a dark army green. *Service:* France, Belgium, Germany and occupation duty.

6th Army Corps variations
Left: Standard type with olive drab border - $20.00. **Right:** Standard type without a border - $5.00. *Service:* Italy, France, Germany, Austria and occupation duty.

8th Army Corps
Standard type - $6.00. *Service:* France, Belgium, Germany.

7th Army Corps variations (1st style, worn until 1944)
Both are standard types with factory variations in size - $6.00.

9th Army Corps variations
Left: Standard type with olive drab border - $20.00. **Right:** Standard type without border - $6.00. *Service:* Philippines and occupation duty in Japan.

12th Army Corps
Standard type - $7.00. *Service:* France, Germany, Luxembourg, Czechoslovakia, Austria and occupation duty in Germany.

10th Army Corps variations
Top left: Standard type with blue border. The blue border variation is scarce - $25.00. **Top right:** Standard type with cross bars omitted. This is somewhat difficult to find - $25.00. **Bottom left:** A very nice theater-made variation. This is embroidered on a diamond-quilted satin background with bullion trim - $60.00. The 10th Corps saw extended service in Korea as well. Consequently, there are numerous theater-made variations from the Philippines, Japan and Australia, dating from WWII, and others originating from Korea during the 1950s. The construction characteristics of this one suggest that it is probably of Korean manufacture. **Bottom right:** Standard type - $6.00. *Service:* Philippines, Australia, New Guinea, and occupation duty in Japan.

13th Army Corps
Standard type - $5.00. *Service:* France, Belgium, Holland, Germany.

11th Army Corps variations
Left: Standard 2nd style with small dots on the dice - $5.00. **Middle:** Standard 2nd style with large dots - $15.00 **Right:** This is the 1st style patch worn prior to WWII - $45.00. *Service:* New Guinea, Morotai Island, Philippines and occupation duty in Japan.

14th Army Corps
Standard type - $6.00. *Service:* Solomon Islands, New Georgia, Philippines.

15th Army Corps (1st and 2nd style)

Left: Standard type, 1st style 15th Corps patch. This is a reproduction produced with nylon threads. This patch is soft and pliable. It has the appearance of being used and old, but the white portions react brilliantly to ultraviolet light, thus identifying it as a fake. There is also a conspicuous absence of snow on the reverse side $2.00. This is a classic example of a reproduction patch. This insignia was used on an unofficial basis for about 10 years, ending in 1943. There is no legitimate use for a more recently produced example. The sole purpose for recent manufacture of this patch, is for sale to collectors. Unfortunately, patches are seldom identified as reproductions. This one was advertised as original. I purchased it specifically for inclusion in this book. For an original $350.00+. **Right:** Standard 2nd style type - $6.00. *Service:* France, Germany, Austria and occupation duty.

16th Army Corps
Standard type - $6.00. *Service:* Germany, Belgium, military government duties in Germany.

Reproduction first style 15th Corps patch in reverse

On a vintage example there would be a much heavier concentration of white or green thread (snow) across the back. There are two vintage examples below for comparison.

Reverse side of original corps patches with olive drab borders

This shows how the reverse sides of WWII period patches normally appear. Both the 10th and 6th Corps patches have an olive drab border. The heavy white and green "snow" on these patches helps in verifying that they are period pieces.

18th Army Airborne Corps / 18th Army Corps

Left: Standard type with separate tab - $8.00. This corps was not designated as an airborne corps until after its arrival in England, in 1944. The existing patch was rotated to the left, so that the dragon was looking down, as if from the sky, and the tab was added over the patch. **Right:** Standard type - $5.00. Examples exist with a right facing dragon, which is the result of the "combat patch" practice. Personnel who had wartime service with a former unit are authorized to wear that unit's patch on the right shoulder. A right shoulder version of this patch would necessitate turning the dragon so that the profile is worn facing forward as technically required. Some right-facing variations are errors, however, military regulations stated that certain patch designs featuring a profile would be worn with the profile facing the wearer's front (Dexter). The introduction of the "combat patch" practice resulted in patches being worn on the left shoulder, which resulted in profiles facing the wearer's rear. Some patches have been manufactored in limited numbers in right-facing variations to address this detail. However, due to the cost and complexity of manufacturing two opposing versions of each design, the right-facing types have never been mandated by regulations for wear on the left shoulder. Right-facing types tend to be quite scarce.

The 18th Corps patch was worn in the diamond position, with the dragon facing left, until its re-designation as an airborne corps. The 18th Corps was formerly the 18th Armored Corps, and the 2nd Armored Corps prior to that. *Service:* England, Holland, France, Belgium, and Germany. The corps was preparing to proceed to the Pacific when Japan capitulated.

19th Army Corps (3rd style)
This patch was worn later in the war. A common variation of this type is embroidered on felt. This is a standard type - $8.00.

18th Army Corps
Standard 1st style, worn from 1921-1943 - $10.00.

20th Army Corps
Standard type - $8.00. *Service:* France, Germany, Austria and occupation duties.

19th Army Corps variations
Standard types with factory variations. **Left:** Solid white tomahawk. **Right:** Has details added to the tomahawk in blue thread. Either design - $7.00. *Service:* France, Holland, Germany and occupation duty in Germany.

21st Army Corps
Standard type - $6.00. *Service:* France, Germany, Austria and occupation duty.

22nd Army Corps
Standard type - $6.00. *Service:* France, Belgium, Germany, Czechoslovakia and occupation duties.

31st Army Corps (phantom)
Standard type - $40.00. *Service:* Ghost/phantom, Operation Fortitude.

23rd Army Corps
Standard type - $6.00. *Service:* France and occupation duty.

33rd Army Corps (phantom)
Standard type - $45.00. *Service:* Ghost/phantom unit, Operation Fortitude.

24th Army Corps
Standard type - $6.00. *Service:* Admiralty Islands, Philippines, Ryukyus Islands, Okinawa, Korea.

36th Army Corps
Standard type - $5.00. *Service:* United States.

ARMY SERVICE COMMANDS

Prior to WWII, the United States was divided into several military districts under corps-level administration. As war became a reality, these corps staffs were required for overseas assignments and were replaced by the service commands. Originally, the service command patches were to be produced in white on an olive drab background. This was later changed to white on a blue background. There is some confusion as to why the color change took place. Research suggests that because the service commands were created to relieve the combat elements of the corps, they would use the flag colors of a corps (blue and white) for their patch designs.

THEATER OF OPERATIONS:
Service commands were responsible for logistics, support, training, and domestic military affairs. They served in the United States with the exceptions of the Northwest Service Command, which served in Canada and Alaska, and the Persian Gulf Service Command, which served in Iran and Iraq. There were 11 service commands and 14 primary patch designs, with several variations known to exist including olive drab borders and olive drab backgrounds. Service commands were unique to the Second World War.

1st Service Command (2nd style)

Standard type - $300.00. The old style patch is quite rare because it was only worn for a couple of months in 1941. From my experience and research, there seems to be a roughly equal proportion of these patches manufactured with and without an olive drab border. This example has no border, but has green snow on the reverse side. An earlier design is identical except that the rectangle and border are olive drab instead of blue - $300.00.

1st Service Command (3rd style)

Standard type, 3rd style - $5.00. *Service:* Responsible for Connecticut, Maine, Massachusetts, New Hampshire, Rhode Island and Vermont.

3rd Service Command
Standard type - $5.00. *Service:* Responsible for Delaware, Maryland, Pennsylvania, Virginia, and Washington, DC.

6th Service Command
Standard type- $5.00. *Service:* Responsible for Illinois, Wisconsin, and Michigan.

4th Service Command
Standard type - $5.00. *Service:* Responsible for Florida, Alabama, Georgia, North Carolina, South Carolina, Mississippi, and Tennessee.

7th Service Command variations
Left: This is an earlier style, embroidered on wool. The wool is commonly found in both black and blue. No explanation for these variations can be offered, but they may be "private purchase" items. It has been suggested that the black version was worn by officers. There is photographic evidence that contradicts this theory - $15.00.
Right: Standard type - $5.00. *Service:* Responsible for Colorado, Kansas, Iowa, Minnesota, Missouri, Nebraska, North Dakota, South Dakota, and Wyoming.

5th Service Command
Standard type - $5.00. One error variation of the Fifth features reversed colors. *Service:* Responsible for West Virginia, Ohio, Kentucky, and Indiana.

8th Service Command
Standard type - $5.00. *Service:* Responsible for Texas, Louisiana, New Mexico, Arkansas, and Oklahoma.

9th Service Command variations
Left: Standard type with olive drab border - $15.00. This is the only service command (with the exception of the rare, 1st style, 1st Service Command, that is commonly found with an olive drab border. Any other service commands found with an olive drab border bring much higher prices - $30.00+. **Right:** Standard type - $5.00. *Service:* Responsible for Oregon, California, Idaho, Arizona, Montana, Nevada, Utah, and Washington.

Persian Gulf Service Command variations
Left: Standard type - $8.00. **Right:** This is a very nice example produced in Iran. This is a standard patch that has been embellished with silver bullion thread. An exceptionally attractive theater-made piece - $65.00. *Service:* Iraq and Iran. It later became a theater of operations and then, once again, was re-designated as a service command. The command's responsibilities included the administration of lend lease to the Russians.

Northwest Service Command
Standard type - $8.00. *Service:* Responsible for the ALCAN (Alaska-Canada) Highway. As a tribute to Canadian participation with this project, the color red was added to the usual blue and white design.

London Base Command (LBC)
Standard type - $15.00. *Service:* The London Base Command was something of an anomaly. Despite being officially designated as a base command, it was not charged with the defensive role commonly associated with a base command. The LBC was directed by the Service of Supply, and its purpose and duties were consistent with that of a service command.

MISCELLANEOUS HEADQUARTERS & COMMANDS (DOMESTIC)

Army Ground Forces

Left: Embroidered type with a horizontal weave and very narrow border - $6.00. *Right:* Standard embroidered type - $3.00. *Service:* The mission of the Army Ground Forces was to provide soldiers that were properly prepared for military operations. This included a range of training from boot camp to highly specialized subjects. This command had an awesome responsibility and it performed far above expectations.

General Headquarters Reserves variations

Left: Fully embroidered with olive drab border and unusually silky thread - $8.00. **Middle:** Fully embroidered with olive drab border - $6.00. **Right:** Standard fully embroidered type - $3.00. *Service:* This command controlled non-divisional, combat-ready forces. Initially, many of the non-divisional personnel were the result of converting "square" divisions (four regiments) to "triangular" divisions (three regiments), which left roughly one regiment per division unassigned and available for duty elsewhere

Army Ground Forces Replacement Depots

Standard type - $5.00. AGF Replacement Depots were established on both coasts. They were responsible for processing combat troops awaiting transport overseas.

Replacement and School Command

Standard type with olive drab border - $3.00. *Service:* Responsible for schools and replacement training centers. It conducted training for the infantry, artillery, cavalry, armored, and tank destroyer forces among others.

Army Service Forces variations

Top row - left: Embroidered on felt, with minor moth nips - $10.00. **Middle:** Fully embroidered in unusually thick, soft threads with circular pattern to weave - $8.00. **Right:** Fully embroidered with white border and circular pattern to weave - $20.00. **Bottom row - left:** Fully embroidered with circular pattern to weave - $5.00. **Right:** Fully embroidered with live drab border, circular pattern to weave, and thick green thread covering the reverse - $15.00. *Service:* Originally the Services of Supply, The army Service Forces managed the army's logistics. The scope of this responsibility is beyond comprehension. The command trained, transported, and supplied millions of soldiers all over the world. A mission they accomplished with magnificent success.

Army Service Forces Training Center Units

Standard design - $5.00. *Service:* The Training Center operated 34 training facilities specializing in technical and administrative services. These units fell under the immediate control of the service commands, which is symbolized by the blue and white.

Ports of Embarkation variations

Left: Scarce embroidered type with concentric circle detail on the ship wheel - $35.00. *Right*: Standard embroidered type - $6.00. *Service:* The Ports of Embarkation were under the authority of the Transportation Corps. They controlled the preparation, storage, and shipping of supplies and personnel. Eventually, its personnel operated from ports in Boston, New York, Hampton Roads, Charleston, New Orleans, Los Angeles, San Francisco, and Seattle.

John Richardson of Andover, New York wearing the ASF patch 1945

My Uncle, John Richardson, who served in North Africa, the Mediterranean, and Europe. During his wartime service he was assigned to the ASF, Ports of Embarkation, and ETO Communications Zone. This photo was taken in the parlor of his parent's home during his first leave.

ANTIAIRCRAFT COMMANDS

Antiaircraft commands were established during WWII and were charged with the responsibility for air defense of the continental United States.

Antiaircraft Command variations

These are all standard types with some subtle variations. Like fingerprints, each patch manufacturer left a unique "signature" of some kind on their patches. Whether it is the texture, the detail, the border, the weave, the material, or perhaps the pattern of "snow" on the reverse, they are seldom identical. In this case, the boldness of the "AA" details varies from patch to patch. If collectors consider subtle differences like these to be variations, the number of variations from WWII are beyond calculation. Any of the above designs - $5.00. *Service:* Operated a number of facilities specializing in antiaircraft, coast artillery, and barrage balloons. This unit conducted its operations within the United States.

Antiaircraft Command (Southern)

Standard type - $7.00. *Service:* Responsible for everything south of North Carolina, Tennessee, Arkansas, and west to include Texas, Oklahoma, and New Mexico.

Antiaircraft Command (Eastern)

Standard type - $5.00. *Service:* Responsible for the Northeast, to include the area from New England to North Carolina, west to the Mississippi, and south to Kentucky.

14th Antiaircraft Command

Standard type - $30.00. Another common variation exists, which is embroidered on felt. This patch can be found with accompanying sub-unit tabs, and also with three "A"'s instead of the normal two. *Service:* The 14th AA Command served as a training and administrative headquarters for antiaircraft units in the Pacific. It was essentially a pool of resources which could be accessed by other units when the need arose, and a home for these resources when they were not actively deployed. Elements from this unit participated in every significant campaign in the southwest Pacific.

Antiaircraft Command (Central)

Standard type - $7.00. *Service:* Responsible for Colorado, Iowa, Kansas, Minnesota, Missouri, Nebraska, the Dakotas', and Wyoming

49th Antiaircraft Artillery Brigade

Standard type - $35.00. Many variations of this patch exist including examples produced in France, England and Germany. *Service:* France, Belgium, Germany and occupation duties.

COAST ARTILLERY

The Coast Artillery Districts were formed prior to WWII and were re-designated a few times prior to being inactivated at the end of the war. They were primarily responsible for the defense of shore-lines, harbor facilities, and the training and readiness of coast artillery personnel. The districts were numbered to correspond with the army corps responsible for their respective regions. The gold and scarlet colors used in these patch designs are the official colors of the coast artillery.

1st Coast Artillery variations
Left: Standard type - $10.00. Although not visible here, this patch has a very distinct vertical weave pattern. **Right:** This is a relatively scarce variation on khaki, for wear on the summer uniform - $25.00. *Service:* Responsible for the northeast boundary of the United States. Its area of responsibility extended as far south as the Nantucket Shoals Lightship.

3rd Coast Artillery
Standard type - $10.00. *Service:* Responsible for the area South of Delaware to North Carolina.

2nd Coast Artillery
Standard type - $10.00. *Service:* Responsible for the coastline stretching from the Nantucket Shoals Lightship to the southern border of Delaware.

4th Coast Artillery
Standard type - $10.00. *Service:* Responsible for North Carolina to the Rio Grande River.

9th Coast Artillery variations

Standard types with subtle variations in design. **Left:** This patch has a circular ribbed weave, a more yellow than gold star, and a narrow projectile. **Right:** This example has a prominent concentration of thread around the edge, the star is a gold, and the projectile is thick and bold. Either type - $10.00. *Service:* Responsible for the west coast, from Canada to Mexico.

Hawaiian Coast Artillery Brigade (Separate)

Standard type - $8.00. *Service:* Responsible for the defense of the Hawaiian Islands.

Hawaiian Coastal Defense

Standard type - $25.00. This organization was formed in response to the Japanese attack on Pearl Harbor, and in anticipation of Japanese invasion which seemed likely at the time. As the war progressed the unit was disbanded and its personnel were dispersed to other units.

DOMESTIC DEFENSE COMMANDS

Eastern Defense Command

This is a standard type - $6.00. *Service:* was responsible for defending the eastern United States, in the event of an invasion.

Western Defense Command

This is a standard type - $5.00. Many variations in the sun detail exist. *Service:* was responsible for defending the western United States in the event of invasion.

Southern Defense Command

This is a standard type - $12.00. *Service:* was responsible for defending the southern United States in the event of an invasion.

Three variations of the 1st style Alaska Defense Command

Left: Fully embroidered with unusual blue sky, buff border, and buff and yellow northern lights - $45.00. **Middle:** Embroidered on twill with red white and blue letters- $45.00. **Right:** Fully embroidered with variation in color and size - $45.00. This design was unauthorized. *Service:* This unit was primarily charged with the defense of Alaska and training.

Alaskan Department variations

These are all fully embroidered examples - $4.00. Myriad variations in facial detail exist. Some have no black at all other than the eyes and nose. *Service:* The department was responsible for defense, training, and overseeing logistical matters that became increasingly complex with lend-lease to Russia.

The Hawaiian Department

Standard fully embroidered type - $4.00. *Service:* Originally the unit was responsible for defending Oahu against Japanese invasion.

U.S. Forces in the Aleutian Islands

This is a standard embroidered on twill type with mesh backing - $35.00. The patch may have been worn by forces stationed at the numerous outposts in the Aleutians during the war. It was an unauthorized design and little official information exists.

Panama "Hellgate" and Panama Canal Department variations

Left: The Panama Hellgate patch was worn by units responsible for the defense of the Canal Zone - $20.00. This is thought to have been a subordinate command to the Panama Canal Department. **Middle:** Standard Panama Canal Department patch - $4.00. **Right:** Panama Canal Department patch with attached "Panama" tab - $15.00. *Service:* Responsible for defending the Panama Canal prior to the war and continued in that role when war broke out.

ARMY DIVISIONS
(INFANTRY / AIRBORNE / CAVALRY)

The army infantry division of WWII was organized differently than its predecessors. These modified formations were referred to as "triangular" divisions. Reliable transport, increased firepower and other factors made it possible to maneuver and fight more effectively with three regiments, rather than the four-Regiment (square) division of WWI. The 1930's and 1940's saw other organizational innovations as well. Many of these new ideas were directed at achieving a more unified and cohesive application of ground and air forces in tactical operations. Military officials around the world were awed by first-hand accounts of the incredible effectiveness of the German armed forces. Observers reported that the Germans had perfected the integration of infantry, armor, mechanized transport, artillery, and air support. This resulted in highly mobile, self-sufficient combat groups. Perfection of this technique eluded the U.S. forces during WWII. Strides were made However, toward achieving a true combat team concept which has become an effective organizational component of the army. The term "triangular division" meant that the primary divisional force consisted of three regiments. Divisions usually had artillery, special weapons, mechanized assets, medical, aviation, and engineer support of their own. But other special needs were met by borrowing from pools of corps and army level resources. An infantry division consisted of roughly, 14,000 troops and 92 divisions were organized during the war. **Armored and cavalry division** information is included in this section. The divisions are the largest "set" of American WWII, authorized army insignia. There are countless variations that can be found. Many of the WWII divisional insignia designs were introduced during WWI and several of these are still in use today.

Abbreviation Key: AB = Airborne Cav = Cavalry Mtn = Mountain Regt = Regiment

THEATER OF OPERATION:

European Theater of Operation (For purposes of this book, includes Africa and the Mediterranean): 1st, 2nd, 3rd, 4th, 5th, 8th, 9th, 10th Mtn, 13th AB, 17th AB, 26th, 28th, 29th, 30th, 31st, 34th, 35th, 36th, 42nd, 44th, 45th, 63rd, 65th, 66th, 69th, 70th, 71st, 75th, 76th, 78th, 79th, 80th, 82nd AB, 83rd, 84th, 85th, 86th, 88th, 89th, 90th, 91st, 92nd, 94th, 95th, 97th, 99th, 100th, 101st AB, 102nd, 103rd, 104th, 106th, 1st Armored, 2nd Armored, 3rd Armored, 4th Armored, 5th Armored, 6th Armored, 7th Armored, 8th Armored, 9th Armored, 10th Armored, 11th Armored, 12th Armored, 13th Armored, 14th Armored, 20th Armored, 2nd Cav.

Pacific Theater of Operation: 6th, 7th, 10th Mtn (87th Regt.-Aleutian Islands), 11th AB, Americal, 24th, 25th, 27th, 32nd, 33rd, 37th, 38th, 40th, 41st, 43rd, 77th, 81st, 86th, 93rd, 96th, 97th, 98th, Philippine Division, 1st Cav.

American Theater of Operation: The 15th, 17th 18th and 19th Armored Divisions were not activated but patches were manufactured during the war. The 3rd Cav, 21st Cav, 24th Cav, 61st Cav, 62nd Cav, 63rd Cav, 64th Cav, 65th Cav, 66th Cav (divisions), and 56th Cav (brigade) were not themselves active, but most of their personnel were active with other units.

Note: The 86th and 97th Divisions were the only two that saw active service in both the European and Pacific Theaters. The 97th Infantry Regiment served in the Aleutians prior to embarking for Europe with the 10th Mountain Division.

Operation Fortitude (ghost/phantom divisions) 6th AB, 9th AB, 11th, 14th, 17th AB, 18th AB, 21st AB, 22nd, 46th, 48th, 50th, 55th, 59th, 108th AB, 119th, 130th, 135th AB, 141st, 157th. These units were part of the deception program known as Operation Fortitude. This involved the creation, on paper, of one army (14th), two corps (31st & 34th) and nineteen divisions. The deception program was incredibly complex. Additionally, the formation of these units was "leaked" to Axis agents and insignia for these units were approved and manufactured to add to the affect. These original insignia are quite scarce, but are a necessary facet of the complete collection.

Service Locations: Each patch description will be accompanied by a brief history of its WWII service. These include countries and locations where they trained, debarked, fought, or otherwise congregated as a unit. Some notations may include specific island(s) where notable engagements occurred, while others may mention just the island group(s), or country(s) where the unit was engaged in operations.. These histories are not intended to be comprehensive and complete. They are simply a synopsis to help collectors and historians when researching the provenance and origin of insignia.

1st Cavalry

Left: WWII standard type - $5.00. **Right:** Current issue patch with army green border indicating post-1957 manufacture - $3.00. This and the 2nd Cavalry Division design are the largest, authorized American division patches. One explanation is that the size and bright color allowed the patch to be distinguishable through the dust inherently generated by horses on the move. *Service:* Australia, New Guinea, Philippines, occupation duty in Japan until being sent to Korea when war broke out there. This patch can also be found with the horse facing right.

1st Cavalry patches in reverse.

Note the heavy white thread ("snow") on the back of the WWII patch (left), and the conspicuous absence of snow on the back of the current patch. This is probably the most fundamental characteristic that WWII patch collectors need to be aware of.

1st Infantry Division

Which of these 1st Infantry Division patches is WWII? The answer is neither. *Left:* This patch is olive drab, which might suggest to a novice collector that it is WWII vintage. However, closer inspection reveals a merrowed edge. Therefore it was probably manufactured after 1968 - $1.00. *Right:* Although this patch has the army green background, it is the older of the two. The army green dates this patch as post-1957, but the edges are cut rather than merrowed. Therefore the patch can be roughly dated between 1957 and 1968 - $1.00. For a WWII fully embroidered type - $5.00. *Service:* Algeria, Sicily, France, Belgium, Germany, Czechoslovakia. This patch can be found with the "1" facing right.

2nd Cavalry Division

Left: Early 2nd Cavalry patch in silky, ribbed weave without olive drab border. This is an example of a patch that is very difficult to find *without* a border - $75.00. *Right:* Standard type - $6.00. The 1st and 2nd Second Cavalry designs are the largest authorized division patches. *Service:* Algeria.

1st Expeditionary Infantry Division of the Brazilian Expeditionary Force

Although this is a Brazilian unit, it had very close association with the American Fifth Army, and is pictured in many U.S. insignia books. After Brazil declared war in 1943, this division was organized and dispatched to Italy, arriving in 1944. The division fought under the direction of the American IV Corps. Several patch designs are known to have been used by this unit. All of them are considered to be rare. *Top:* This patch is the type most commonly associated with the division, embroidered on felt - $350.00. *Bottom:* Italian made, oversized tab-style patch with bullion trim - $200.00.

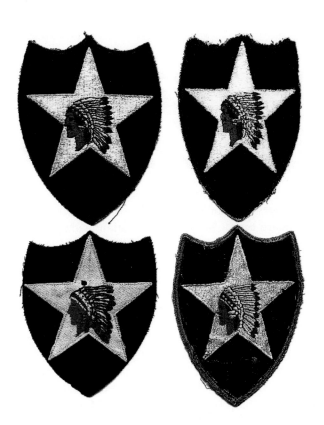

2nd Infantry Division variations

Top left: Standard type - $6.00. *Top right:* Standard type with narrower body - $6.00. *Botton left:* 1930s type with the Indian head embroidered on a white wool star. The star is applied to a black wool base - $50.00. *Bottom right:* Fully embroidered with an olive drab border and heavy green "snow" on the back - $45.00. Many variations of the Indian head detail exist. Some can be found with no facial details at all. Another variation exists with the Indian's head facing right. *Service:* France, Germany, Czechoslovakia.

3rd Cavalry

This is a standard fully embroidered design in unused condition - $10.00. *Service:* Was not activated as a unit in WWII.

3rd Infantry Division variations

Left: German made, coarse weave $5.00. **Middle:** Standard type - $4.00. **Right:** Italian made. The blue stripes are printed on silk - $12.00. The 3rd Division is an example of a patch that can be found in North African, Italian, French, English, and German- made variations. It was an unusually well traveled combat unit. A collector could spend a lifetime just assembling different patches from this division. Although it is little mentioned, North Africa was the source of many theater made insignia. Egypt, specifically, was a source for some of the most beautiful hand embroidery in the world. *Service:* North Africa, French Morocco, Sicily, France, Germany and Austria.

4th Infantry Division variations

Top left: Standard type - $4.00. **Top middle:** Oversized variation - $8.00. **Top right:** German made embroidered variation. The background is lighter than the U.S. olive drab designs - $6.00. **Bottom left:** German tailor made, embroidered on officer's quality uniform material. The edges are folded on the backside - $12.00. **Bottom middle:** This is the hardest U.S. fully embroidered variation to find. Note that the leaves point to the flat sides of the patch rather then the corners - $25.00. **Bottom right:** Current type with merrowed edge. The 4th ID is one of the patch designs where the entire background color was changed when the army made the transition to the army green uniform. The lighter tan color provides better contrast on the dark green uniform - $1.00. *Service:* France, Belgium, Germany.

5th Infantry Division variations

Left: Standard type type with olive drab border. The bordered design is slightly less common than the borderless design $7.00. **Middle:** Oversize variation with white border. There are several theories as to what the white border signifies, but I have yet to see anything conclusive. These are often advertised as a WWII period variant, but they are more likely from the Korean War era - $10.00. *Right:* Standard type - $3.00. *Service:* France, Germany, Czechoslovakia.

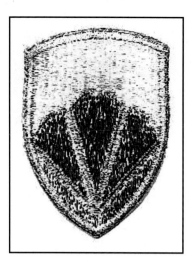

6th Airborne Division in reverse showing heavy white "snow"

Most reproductions will not have heavy concentrations of "snow" on the back. *Service:* Ghost/phantom, Operation Fortitude.

6th Division variations

Left: Standard type with olive drab border - $7.00. **Middle:** Standard type without border - $3.00. **Right:** Standard type with a looser weave (may have been made in the Philippines) and smaller than normal - $5.00. *Service:* Defensive duty Hawaii, New Guinea, Dutch New Guinea, Philippines and occupation duty in Korea.

6th Airborne Division (phantom)

Standard type: $75.00. Aside from the 135th Airborne, the original 6th Airborne is the most difficult fully embroidered WWII division patch to find. The market is flooded with reproductions of "ghost" or "phantom" designs. Reproductions in 100% cotton are common, so the UV light test offers no certainty. When shopping for original ghost patches, look for signs of age, quality construction and heavy "snow" on the reverse. With some experience period patches will be easy to differentiate from fakes.

7th Infantry Division variations

Left: Standard type with olive drab border - $5.00. **Right:** Standard type without border - $25.00. The 7th Division is an example of a patch that is more desirable without the border. *Service:* Aleutian Islands, Marshall Islands, Philippines, and Okinawa.

8th Infantry Division variations
Left: Standard type with olive drab border - $8.00 **Middle:** Standard type without border - $4.00. **Right:** Standard type with accompanying airborne tab - $12.00. The airborne examples are often represented as being WWII, which is incorrect. Elements of the 509th Parachute Infantry Regiment were attached to the 8th ID in the late 50s and early 60s. This is a post-Korean War patch configuration worn by those elements. *Service:* France, Luxembourg, Germany.

Ultra rare 9th Infantry Division variation.
The patch and tabs are German made. The patch is embroidered and embellished with bullion. The tabs are embroidery and bullion on blue felt. This patch / tab combination was worn by members of the 39th Infantry Regiment. The "AAA-O" stands for Anything, Anytime, Anywhere, bar nothing. This is an ultra rare patch and tab combination - $400.00. *Service:* Algiers, Morocco, Sicily, France, Belgium and Germany.

PFC Billy Rozakis, Brooklyn New York, wearing the 8th Division patch, 1944

9th Infantry Division
Standard type - $4.00

9th Airborne Division (phantom)
This is another original ghost division patch with original tab - $45.00+. *Service:* Ghost/phantom, Operation Fortitude.

is commonly found with an attached (integral) tab, and with uncut material in the arch between the tab and patch.

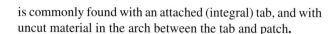

10th Mountain Division

Standard type with tab - $6.00. *Service:* Aleutian Islands (one regiment), Italy.

12th Infantry Division (Philippine) variations

Left: Standard type - $8.00. **Right:** Philippine made variation, which is hand embroidered on twill - $20.00. *Service:* The entire division was "lost in action" during the defense of the Philippines.

11th Infantry Division (ghost/phantom)

This is a standard type - $30.00. *Service:* Ghost/phantom, Operation Fortitude.

Philippine made 12th Division in reverse

11th Airborne Division

Standard type with separate tab - $8.00. *Service:* New Guinea, Philippines and occupation duty in Japan. The 11th

13th Airborne Division variations

Left: Standard type with integral tab and no border - $8.00. **Middle:** Standard type with separate tab

and olive drab border. Although they came as a set, the tab shown is incorrect for the patch - $7.00. *Right:* Variation standard type with less defined details and the color is more yellow than gold. This also has the integral tab and no border - $8.00. Many variations in detail exist. There is no appreciable difference in value with or without a border. *Service:* Elements of the 13th saw action in France and Central Europe but the division was never committed as a unit.

17th Airborne Division variations
Left: Standard patch with variation in detail. Note that the tips of the middle two talons turn toward each other - $25.00. **Right:** Standard type with blue felt added to the back and sky blue thread embellishment around the edges. The added blue detail adds to aesthetic interest, but does not have any appreciable effect on value - $6.00. Both of these have separate tabs. Integral tab types are common as well. A scarce variation exists without an olive drab border. *Service:* France, Luxembourg, Germany and occupation duties.

14th Infantry Division (phantom)
Standard type - $40.00. *Service:* Ghost / phantom, Operation Fortitude.

17th Infantry Division (phantom)
This is a standard type - $40.00. Ghost / phantom, Operation Fortitude.

18th Airborne Division (phantom)
This is a quality reproduction. The vendor put an authentic tab with it to make it even harder to detect as a fake. Someone went to even further extremes by soaking this patch in diluted coffee. Patches soaked in coffee will assume a soiled, more aged appearance. However, the patch is rigid and not as supple as a 55-year old patch should be. There is minimal "snow" on the reverse and a clear glue-like substance (sizing) covers a good deal of the reverse side be-

tween threads. This application of sizing suggests post-1946 manufacture. This patch is all cotton and cannot be detected as a reproduction with UV light. For an original $35.00. For a reproduction $ 2.00. *Service:* Ghost / phantom. Operation Fortitude.

22nd Infantry Division (phantom) *front and back.*

Standard type - $50.00. There are primarily two variations of this patch. The patch shown is known as the "fat" scorpion, and another type exists with a noticeably skinnier scorpion. *Service:* Ghost / phantom, Operation Fortitude. This is what collectors should look for when searching for a genuine WWII patch. This patch is thick, quality construction. The colored threads are applied liberally. The khaki base material is visible at the cut edges. The colors are bright, but the patch *looks* older. It is interesting to note that this was a ghost unit and the patch was never issued or worn. Nevertheless, the patch doesn't *look* new. Further evidence of age appears in the form of moth nips visible around the upper claw. Although not all factory embroidered WWII patches had this degree of white thread ("snow") covering the back, they did have some, and particularly around the highest points on the reverse side and edge.

21st Airborne Division (phantom)

This is a standard type - $45.00. *Service:* Ghost / phantom, Operation Fortitude.

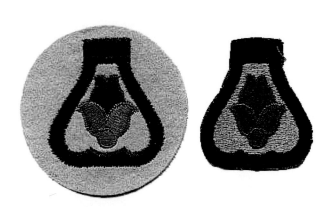

21st Cavalry Division variations

Left: This is a pre-war design, embroidered on a yellow wool disc - $25.00. **Right:** Standard fully embroidered type - $15.00. Variations in the shade of purple can be found. *Service:* Not active as a unit.

23rd Infantry Division (Americal)

Standard type $5.00. *Service:* New Caledonia, Guadalcanal, Fiji Islands, Solomon Islands, Philippines and occupation duty in Japan. "Americal" was the official name designation of this division. This patch was later authorized for wear by the 23rd Division.

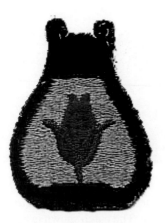

24th Cavalry Division

Standard type - $15.00. Like the 21st Cavalry, this patch can be found embroidered on a wool disc - $25.00. *Service:* Was not activated as a unit.

variations of this patch can be found from the 1920's and 30's, when this unit was officially known as the Hawaiian Division. Several sizes and configurations are known to exist. One interesting variation is applied to a domed, metal backing and is normally advertised as being for wear on the pith helmet. Actually, the metal domed types were frequently worn on the uniform jacket and could be removed easily for laundering. Most earlier designs are felt on felt construction. This patch can be found with a "AIRBORNE" tab. The correct tab is red letters on a black tab. The Airborne design is post- WWII, and fairly scarce. *Service:* (Formerly, Hawaiian Division). Hawaii, Dutch New Guinea, Philippines and occupation duty in Japan.

Hawaiian Division

This is a good quality reproduction. It is detected by examining the back, which has almost no "snow", and a coating of opaque, glue-like substance - $2.00. For an original - $30.00. *Service:* This design was used until 1941. See the 23rd Division below for the unit's wartime service.

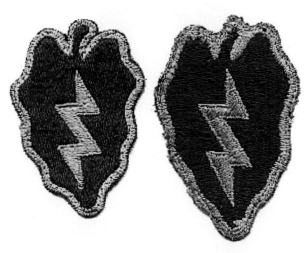

25th Infantry Division variations

Left: Philippine made variation with a looser weave and feels very stiff - $12.00. *Right:* Standard type - $4.00. *Service:* Hawaiian defense, Solomon Islands, and the Philippines.

24th Infantry Division variations

Note the difference in border width and the yellow outline on the leaf. For any standard embroidered type - $5.00. Many

26th Infantry Division variations

Left: Embroidered on khaki twill for summer wear - $20.00. **Right:** Standard type with olive drab background

- $5.00. There are several WWII patches that were produced on khaki for wear on the khaki uniform. In almost every case, the khaki variations are harder to find. *Service:* France, Luxembourg, Germany, Austria and Czechoslovakia.

27th Infantry Division variations
Left: High quality standard type with olive drab border. This example is unusually thick. In this case, the olive drab border is more difficult to find then the version without a border - $15.00. **Middle:** Japanese made variation, embroidered on black felt - $25.00. **Right:** Classic "Studley" type. Studley produced full sized and miniature renditions of WWI patches, throughout the 1940's. The background colors vary and both wool and felt were used. Studley types are frequently mistaken for theater made/unusual variations. The miniature types were marketed to WWI veterans for wear on veteran's association caps. - $12.00. One example exists with the division patch design embroidered on a khaki disc., probably for wear on the summer uniform - $50.00. *Service:* Defense of Hawaiian Islands, elements of this division saw action in the Gilbert Islands, Mariana Islands and occupation duty in Japan.

29th Infantry Division
Standard type - $5.00. Interestingly, events can create temporary surges of interest in a particular unit insignia. The incredible film *Saving Private Ryan* generated an overnight demand for the diamond shaped Ranger patch and the 29th Division patch. Do not fall prey to temporary "hype"- driven pricing trends. I have seen standard 29th Division patches selling for as much as $35.00 dollars on internet auctions. The 29th is a common patch. It can be found at flea markets, junk shops, military shows and antique shops for $1.00. The absolute maximum market value for a WWII, fully embroidered example is $6.00. *Service:* France, Germany and occupation duties.

30th Infantry Division variations
Left: Oversize variation with thick blue border - $10.00. **Middle:** Standard type variation with red border - $20.00. **Right:** Standard type - $5.00. Members of this division are known to have worn this patch in a vertical and horizontal manner. Vertical is the correct method of wear. *Service:* France, Belgium, Holland, Germany and occupation duty.

28th Infantry Division variations
Left: Standard type - $5.00. **Right:** Standard type with olive drab border - $8.00. *Service:* France, Luxembourg, Germany and occupation duties.

31st Infantry Division variations
Left: Standard type with olive drab border - $10.00.
Middle: Standard type with white border - $20.00. **Right:**
Most common standard type - $5.00. *Service:* New Guinea,
Spice Islands, and Philippines.

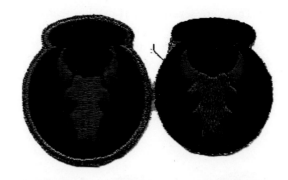

34th Infantry Division variations
Right: Standard type with olive drab border - $12.00. **Right:**
Standard type - $5.00. *Service:* Algiers, Tunisia, and Italy.

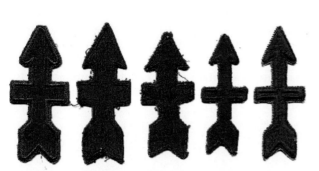

32nd Infantry Division variations
This is a good illustration of the myriad variations existing in American, fully embroidered (standard type) patches. **Left:** Standard type with olive drab border - $10.00.
Second – fifth: Are standard embroidered types, but the sizes vary depending on the manufacturer - $5.00. *Service:* New Guinea, Philippines and occupation duties in Japan.

34th Division variations
Left: German-made 34th Division patch. Machine embroidered on gray wool with a white border. This is a very unusual variation - $30.00. **Right:** Another German machine embroidered example. The skull is narrow and well defined. This patch has a black back - $10.00.

33rd Infantry Division variations
Left: Standard type with olive drab border - $25.00. **Right:**
Most common standard type - $5.00. *Service:* Defensive duties in Hawaii, New Guinea, Spice Islands, Philippines.

35th Division
Right: Standard type with "green back" - $5.00. **Right:**
Standard type - $5.00. Over the past few years, collectors have shown a specific interest in patches with green snow on the reverse. These are now commonly referred to as "green back" (GB) variations. Collectors and dealers are associating a higher value with the green back patches. Although green backs are slightly less common than white back types, they are not, by any stretch of the imagination, scarce. Green backs are *usually* found on patches with olive drab borders, but that is not always the case. *Service:* France, Belgium, Luxembourg, Holland, Germany, and occupation duties.

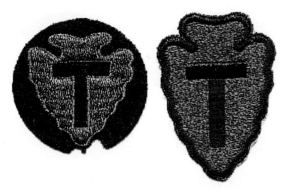

36th Infantry Division variations

Left: Pre-war embroidered on wool type. Note the mothing at the bottom of the patch - $5.00 with moth damage, $10.00 without damage. **Right:** Standard type with olive drab border - $10.00. The most common type has no border. A very scarce fully embroidered variation exists which has a yellow "T" on a dark blue background. Another variation is embroidered on a khaki background for wear on the khaki uniform. *Service:* Africa, Italy, France, and Germany.

39th Infantry Division

Standard type - $6.00. *Service:* Not activated although patches were produced during the war.

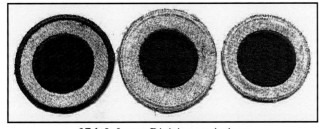

37th Infantry Division variations

Left: Standard type with olive drab border - $8.00. **Middle:** Standard type, unusually large and extra broad white section - $8.00. **Right:** Standard type - $5.00. *Service:* Fiji Islands, Solomon Islands and the Philippines.

40th Infantry Division

Top left: Standard type with olive drab border - $35.00. **Top right:** Standard type - $5.00. **Bottom left:** Gold bullion and tinsel on blue wool. This patch was made in Korea during the Korean War. It is difficult to differentiate between theater-made patches from the Korean War and those from WWII. In this case, even the unit history does not provide much assistance to the collector. The 40th served in the pacific during WWII, spending time in Korea during the Occupation period. Consequently, 1940s Asian made, and specifically Korean-made variations exist. Elements of the 40th also served in Korea during the Korean War and many 40th designs were created during the 50s. So, unless the collector has verification of the patch's provenance, it is anybody's guess. The fact is, regardless of the precise period, the patches are extremely attractive and equally interesting. Whether it is Korean made in the 1940s, or Korean made in

38th Infantry Division

Standard type - $5.00. *Service:* Defense of Gulf Coast, Hawaiian defense, Solomon Islands, and the Philippines.

the 1950s, there is no appreciable difference in worth - $50.00. **Bottom right:** This is the "Ball of Fire" variation. This patch is sometimes mistaken for a WWII design. The "Ball of Fire" patch is Korean-made and dates to the Korean War. There are two plausible theories as to why this patch exists. The first, suggests that the Ball of Fire type distinguished members of the 40th (National Guard Division) cadre from draftees and other personnel that were assigned to the 40th after its arrival in Korea. The second theory is that the Ball of Fire patch was awarded as a badge of courage and was regarded as an honor similar to the Combat Infantryman's Badge within the division. The "Ball of Fire" tab that sometimes accompanies the patch is green with red letters, and occasionally, red trim. Reproductions often have red and yellow accents on the green. The "Ball of Fire" patch may be found in crude Korean-made styles, or factory embroidered. The patch is scarce $150.00. The tab is quite rare $150.00+. *Service:* Hawaiian defense, New Britain, Philippines, Visayan Islands and occupation duties in Korea.

41st Infantry Division variations

Top Left: Pre-war embroidered on wool - $20.00. **Top right:** Pre-war embroidered on wool with slight variation in weave and color - $20.00. **Middle Left:** WWII standard type - $4.00. **Middle Right:** Asian-made example with gold bullion and embroidery on wool base - $45.00. **Bottom Left:** Another embroidered on wool pre-war type - $20.00. **Bottom Right:** Australian Hand embroidered variation - $35.00. Many of the pre-war types are found in use on WWII uniforms. They are larger and more attractive. *Service:* Solomon Islands and the Philippines.

40th Infantry Division "Ball of Fire" variations

Top: Fully embroidered type in unused condition - $125.00. **Bottom:** Another fully embroidered type with a darker yellow and heavier concentration of red thread. This patch was removed from a uniform - $125.00.

1930s period 41st Infantry Division blouse

This blouse has a oversized, hand-embroidered 41st patch and felt on felt sergeant stripes. Note the cross stitching around the patches, which adds a particularly handsome appearance. The enlisted discs are transitional types with a brass color and checkerboard texture. The distinctive insignias (DIs) are screw-back types.

42nd Infantry Division variations
Left: Standard type - $4.00. **Right:** Standard type with heavy ribbed weave appearance - $7.00. *Service:* France, Germany, Austria and occupation duties.

44th Infantry Division variations
Top Left: Standard embroidered type that has been embellished with bullion by a German artisan during the Occupation period. **Top Middle:** Standard type with olive drab border - $20.00. **Top Right:** Standard type - $5.00. **Bottom:** Woven, German-made example in miniature size, probably for wear on an overseas cap - $15.00. *Service:* France, Germany, Austria and occupation duties.

43rd Infantry Division variations
Left: Standard type with olive drab border - $12.00. **Right:** Standard type - $5.00. Another fully embroidered variation exists with a buff colored border. The buff border is very scarce - $30.00. *Service:* New Hebrides, Russell Islands, New Georgia, Solomon Islands, Philippines and occupation duties.

44th Infantry Division patch in reverse
This shows the reverse of the 44th Division patch with olive drab border. Note the green back, which can be found on many WWII patches. Although not scarce, green-back types have become a specific area of interest amongst some collectors.

43rd Division variation
This example has a buff-color border rather than olive drab or, most commonly, no border at all - $30.00.

45th Infantry Division variations
Top left: Standard type - $5.00. **Top right:** Standard type with olive drab border. The olive drab border significantly increases the value of a 45th Division patch - $45.00.

Bottom: This is a felt on felt pre-war example - $50.00. Note a couple moth nips in the background felt. The nips are not significant enough to detract from the appearance or value. The division originally adopted this Native American symbol for their patch. With the outbreak of WWII, the design was discontinued due to its similarity to the swastika used by the Nazi Party. The thunderbird, another Native American symbol, was selected for the new design. The pre-war type can be found worn in the square or diamond configuration. There are a series of pre-war patches that incorporate the swastika on a felt or wool disc. The swastikas vary in color. These patches are frequently attributed to the 45th Division, but they are actually high school RESERVE OFFICER'S TRAINING CORPS patches. The colors identify the particular school. *Service:* North Africa, Sicily, Italy, France, Germany and occupation duties.

45th Division variations

Left: Full embroidered with black base material visible at edges. The owner has added white thread to accent the wing and tail details - $6.00. **Right:** An early, fully embroidered example. This patch is slightly smaller than usual and the phoenix is narrow and particularly simplistic. Note the added eye detail - $10.00.

46th Infantry Division (phantom) variations

Left: This is the correct, standard type - $45.00. **Right:** This variation is the error type - $65.00+. The green and blue were inadvertently reversed by the manufacturer. Some claim that the only producer of the error version was the Patch King. In 1998, I acquired a box of patches from an elderly woman in Medford, Oregon. During WWII, this woman had worked in a textile plant that manufactured insignia amongst other things. She told me that the box of patches were keepsakes she had personally obtained from the plant during her employment there. All of the patches were definitely vintage pieces. Included in the box were 31st and 33rd Army Corps patches (both ghost / phantom units) and a 46th Division error patch. All of the patches in the box were of relatively identical construction and appearance, both front and back. It is possible that she obtained the 46th error type in a box of cereal or a similar scenario, and she dropped it in with her keepsakes from the plant. And, therefore the patch may be a Patch King piece. Memories will certainly fade over 53 years, but the woman insists that the only source she ever obtained a military patch from, was the plant. If that is true, then the 46th error type was produced by other official military sources as well. I have since obtained other period 46th error type examples. I have noted substantial differences in the "snow" on the reverse sides of these patches. If the Patch King was the sole source of this patch, the thread patterns should be relatively consistent. There is a degree of consistency in hundreds of other Patch King patches that I have analyzed over the years. The variation in thread configuration and density on the 46th error patches tends to suggest different manufacturers. *Service:* Ghost / phantom, Operation Fortitude.

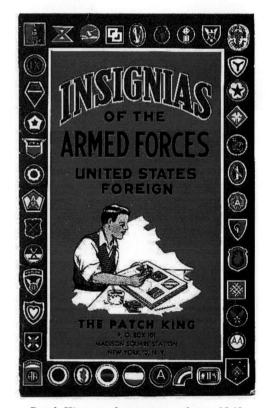

Patch King catalogue cover - latter 1940s

The Patch King was a military insignia supplier during the war. After the war, the company recognized a market for the millions of surplus patches they had produced, and began marketing to collectors. Among other outlets, Patch King patches became a popular novelty item and could be obtained in a number of ways including proof of purchase coupons from various products and as prizes in breakfast cereal. But most were ordered from the company catalogue. Aside from original patches from wartime stockpiles, they also made copies of rare WWII patches and reproduction WWI patches for collectors. Collectors will find that many period patches have glue remnants on the reverse side from having been glued to a board or a scrapbook for display. I have heard lots of collectors and dealers alike commenting on why anyone would damage a patch by gluing it to something. The fact is, the Patch King catalogue cover featured an illustration of a young collector gluing his newest acquisitions into a scrapbook, thus encouraging this technique. The rear page states "Many of our collectors have framed assortments on their walls, or have mounted them in catalogues....". It seemed like a great technique at the time. It would have been difficult at the time to imagine that these "dime-a-dozen" patches, literally stockpiled by the millions, would be worth a small fortune later on. Many collectors rely upon photos and illustrations in period references to assist them in displaying their patches correctly. It is interesting to note that many of the patches illustrated in Patch King catalogues are upside down or otherwise improperly displayed.

48th Infantry Division
This patch is frequently misidentified as a WWII patch or a Ghost / phantom patch. It is actually an authorized division patch for the 48th National Guard Division. The unit was activated in 1949 and deactivated in the early 1950s - $15.00.

47th Infantry Division
The 47th Division was not active during WWII. This example has a cut-edge and was advertised by the seller as being a WWII design. It is actually from the early 1960s.

49th Infantry Division
This is another patch that is frequently represented as being WWII. This unit was not activated until 1946. It is WWII era, but technically is a post-war design - $10.00.

48th Infantry Division (Ghost)
Standard type - $45.00. *Service:* Ghost / phantom, Operation Fortitude.

50th Infantry Division (phantom)
Standard design - $40.00. *Service:* Ghost / phantom, Operation Fortitude.

51st Infantry Division

Yet another patch that is commonly represented as a WWII or Ghost / phantom patch. This unit was activated in 1946 and deactivated a couple of years later. It is a post-war design $20.00.

59th Infantry Division (phantom)

Standard type - $45.00. Another variation exists with no spaces between the coils - $60.00. *Service:* Ghost / phantom, Operation Fortitude.

have a significantly detrimental effect on value these days. Collectors are willing to pay money for original examples as long as the mothing does not detract too much from the overall appearance. I encourage collectors to hold out for patches in very good condition. An extra five dollars for a specimen without mothing will insure your investment continues to appreciate. The exception to this rule would be a patch that is so extraordinarily rare to find in any condition, that even a damaged example is highly desirable. *Service:* Not active as a unit.

62nd Cavalry Division variations.
Left: Embroidered on felt, with moderate moth damage - $20.00. **Right:** Standard type - $15.00. *Service:* Not active as a unit.

61st Cavalry Division

This is a pre-war example, embroidered on wool, with moderate moth damage - $20.00. Light or moderate mothing to most wool patches does not seem to

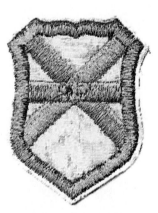

62nd Cavalry Division in reverse

This shows the white muslin commonly used to cover the back of early embroidered on felt / wool Cavalry types. Cheesecloth is also a common backing component.

63rd Cavalry Division variations

Left: Pre-war example, embroidered on felt - $25.00. **Right:** Standard type $12.00. *Service:* Not active as a unit.

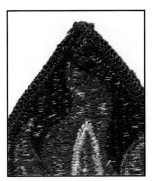

63rd Infantry Division in reverse

This shows the pigtail and the distinctive tire-tread design of a merrowed edge patch. With the exception of one 506th Parachute Infantry Regiment variation, these characteristics are conclusive, irrefutable evidence that the patch was manufactured after 1968.

63rd Infantry Division variations

Left: Current issue type with merrowed edge. Note the high ridge along the edge and the small chain stitch barely visible around the inside of the ridge. These are the characteristics of a merrowed-edge patch. Merrowed patches have a pigtail of thread on the reverse. occasionally, the pigtail is trimmed off, but you can see evidence of where the pigtail was upon close examination. **Right:** This is a German-made patch with added decorative yellow trim around the edge - $20.00. Note the unusual definition around the edges of the flame. This patch can be found with a white sword as well. *Service:* France, Germany and occupation duties.

64th Cavalry Division

This pre-war patch is embroidered on felt - $25.00. *Service:* Not active as a unit.

65th Cavalry Division

This is a standard type - $12.00. *Service:* Not active as a unit.

65th Infantry Division variations

Left: Standard type - $5.00. ***Right:*** Another standard type with subtle variations in size and detail - $5.00. The definition of "variation" varies from one collector to the next. If the collector considers extremely subtle differences in design, like those shown above, the possibilities are endless. *Service:* France, Germany and Austria.

Top left: This is a standard type, second style 66th Division patch - $12.00. This design was adopted in 1943. Apparently, the running cat became the target of derogatory remarks, so an alternative design was proposed. *Top right:* Standard type, first style patch $20.00 *Bottom:* Standard type, first style patch. Note the subtle differences in detail like the eyes, whiskers and nose color - $20.00. *Service:* France and occupation duties.

Old 66th Division variation

Standard type, but note that the cat has no red in it's mouth and that there are no whiskers - $45.00.

66th Cavalry Division

Left: This is a pre-war, embroidered on wool patch, with moderate moth damage - $10.00. **Right:** Standard type - $15.00. *Service:* Not active as a unit.

66th Infantry Division variations

69th Infantry Division

This is a standard type - $6.00. A scarce variation can be found without the white trim around the edge. *Service:* France, Belgium, Germany and occupation duties.

70th Infantry Division variations

Left: German-made, with embroidered details on a stiff, silky background - $25.00. **Middle:** Standard type with olive drab border - $15.00. **Right:** Standard type - $5.00. Note the slight differences in the color and details of the two fully embroidered examples. *Service:* France, Germany and occupation duties.

71st Infantry Division variations

Left: This example has an unusually shiny, silky appearance and may be overseas-made -$5.00 **Right:** A standard type with a more typical appearance - $5.00. *Service:* France, Germany, Austria and occupation duties.

75th Infantry Division

This is a standard type - $5.00. One variation of this patch can be found without the white outlining the numbers. Another exists with no olive drab border. Both of those variations are quite scarce - $45.00. *Service:* France, Belgium, Holland, Germany and occupation duties.

76th Infantry Division

This is a quality, standard design. Many 76th Division patches utilize a true brown shade around the border as opposed to the usual olive drab - $10.00. *Service:* France, Luxembourg, Germany, Czechoslovakia and occupation duties.

77th Infantry Division variations

Left: Standard type, but with the light blue background - $20.00. **Middle:** Standard type - $5.00. **Right:** Standard type with slightly different details - $5.00. Numerous variations exist with differences in the details of the statue. Another rare variation exists with a yellow statue on a green background - $200.00+. *Service:* Guam, Philippines, Okinawa and occupation duties in Japan.

77th Infantry Division in reverse

This shows a white-back and green-back example of the 77th Division patch.

79th Infantry Division

This is a standard type - $5.00. *Service:* France, Belgium, Germany and occupation duties. Some interesting variations of this patch were created overseas during WWII. One variation has a solid sterling silver cross, affixed to a blue felt shield.

77th Infantry Division with olive drab border

The 77th is one of several WWII patches that have a significantly enhanced value when found with an olive drab border. Interestingly, in the normal, borderless type, the light blue is hardest to find. But in the bordered type, a *dark* blue is hardest to find. This particular example has a distinct vertically ribbed weave - $300.00.

Note: Many patches like the 77th can be found in different colors. These odd color variations are frequently attributed to college and high school ROTC programs and are not related to military use.

80th Infantry Division variations

Left: Standard type with light-blue mountains - $5.00. *Right:* Standard type with dark-blue mountains - $15.00. *Bottom:* The Airborne tab worn with the 80th Division (Reserve) patch from 1946-1952. It is a post-war tab. Tabs have become a popular item to reproduce and the market is flooded with them. Many of the reproductions are all cotton, making it impossible to detect them with ultraviolet light. Original 80th tabs alone sell for $25.00+. *Service:* France, Germany, Luxembourg, Belgium, Austria and occupation duties.

78th Infantry Division variations

Left: This is the scarce standard type without an olive drab border - $50.00 *Right:* Standard type - $5.00. Several variations in size can be found. *Service:* France, Belgium, Germany and occupation duty.

81st Division variations

Left: This is a standard type, but rather than white or green "snow" on the back, this patch has black snow - $6.00. **Middle:** Standard type with green snow on the reverse - $6.00. **Right:** This patch has no black border and is the hardest 89th factory variation to find - $30.00. *Service:* West Carolines, Philippines and occupation duties. Although cloth distinctive badges were worn prior to WW I, the 81st is credited with being the first American division to wear a shoulder sleeve insignia. It was just prior to embarking for France in WW I that the 81st adopted this design

Bullion 82nd Airborne Division

English-made example with bullion on a corduroy material. This is a miniature design intended perhaps, for an overseas cap - $65.00.

82nd Airborne Division variations

Left: Standard type with separate tab - $8.00. **Middle:** Standard type with attached tab. Note that the khaki base material between the tab and patch was never removed. This patch can be found with uncut olive drab material as well - $20.00. **Right** Standard type with attached tab - $10.00. The 82nd Division patch with an olive drab border is extremely rare. The last example I saw for sale (1998) sold for - $800.00. *Service:* North Africa, Sicily, Italy, France, Holland, Belgium, Germany and occupation duties.

82nd Airborne jump jacket with staff sergeant chevrons

82nd Airborne Division with olive drab border

This is the extremely rare factory variation with olive drab border - $800.00+.

83rd Infantry Division variations

Left: Standard type - $6.00. **Right:** Standard type with olive drab border - $35.00. Another factory variation can be found with white details rather than yellow - $50.00. *Service:* U.K., France, Luxembourg, Belgium, Germany and occupation duties.

84th Infantry Division

Standard type - $5.00. The airborne tab was worn by the Division (Reserve) from 1946-1952, and is a post-war item. Reproductions of uncommon tabs like this one are being mass produced. Many are all cotton designs and are difficult to identify as reproductions. An aged appearance and signs of use are about all the collector has to rely upon. This tab is an all cotton reproduction. At least 95% of those offered on internet auctions or dealer lists are fakes, but they are fetching authentic prices. Authentic airborne tabs like those belonging to the 84th and 80th Divisions are expensive ($25.00+) so be selective. *Service:* France, Holland, Germany, Belgium and occupation duties.

87th Infantry Division

Standard type - $5.00. *Service:* France, Belgium, Luxembourg and Germany.

88th Infantry Division variations

Left: Italian, hand-made variation for the 913th Field Artillery. The patch is blue twill with silver bullion trim. The tab is blue wool with bullion letters and numbers, and embroidered trim. Numerous variations of this patch and accompanying tabs are known to exist. Some have a devil's head design in the center, which is often done in bullion. The tabs and trim on these variations are also frequently done in bullion and incorporate mottoes including "Blue Devils", and "Italy". Regimental or battalion identifiers are also common like the example shown. These Italian-made patches and tabs can be found in a variety of colors including blue, red, green and yellow. The bullion examples with accompanying tabs (particularly with a devil's head incorporated in the patch design) may be worth $100.00 - $300.00 +. **Right:** Standard type - $5.00. *Service:* French Morocco, Algeria, Italy, Austria and occupation duties in Italy and Trieste.

85th Infantry Division

Standard type - $5.00. *Service:* French Morocco, Algeria, Italy and Austria.

86th Infantry Division

Standard type - $5.00. *Service:* France, Germany, Austria and the Philippines.

88th Division devil's head variation

Italian made, bullion on wool example of the devil's head type. Many variations in detail can be found. Frequently, these patches are accompanied with matching tabs. Text on the tabs includes "BLUE DEVILS", "88th DIVISION", unit identifications and any combination thereof. Devil's head examples are fairly scarce and the prices range from $125.00-$300.00 depending on workmanship and wording on the tab.

89th Infantry Division variations
Left: The full color standard design was not adopted until after WWII - $4.00. **Middle:** Standard type - $5.00 **Right:** Another standard type with a larger green border area - $8.00.

Variations of the 89th Division patch with color inserts include: Regimental colors like: Blue ___/, Red ___/, Orange ___/, Chemical Warfare, cobalt blue and golden yellow ___/ Finance, silver-gray and golden yellow ___/ Medical, maroon and white ___/ Military Police, yellow and green ___/ Quartermaster Corps, buff ___/ Signal Corps, orange and white ___/ Tank Destroyer Forces, orange and black ___/ Ordinance, crimson and yellow ___/ Adjutant General's Dept., dark blue and scarlet ___ . Sanitary Train, red cross in center ___/ Another has a sunflower, which simply symbolized that many of its personnel were from Kansas ___/. This list is not intended to be complete. They are representative of the types collectors are likely to encounter. Many were not recognized by the division but were copied from other patches like the First Army, which also had a color coding system. Some of these are fairy tale variations and original examples do not exist. There are other types and combinations that are not listed here.

89th Infantry Division variations (reproduction)
During WWI, many divisions unofficially identified organic sub-units by changing the shape of the patch or adding colors to the design. The 89th added colors/symbols under the center of the "W" for sub-unit identification. This practice continued to a decreasing extent into the 1940s. These color insert types are scarce and collectible (the predicates for reproducers). These particular examples are reproductions and are embroidered on twill. Some of these designs have white thread on the reverse that reacts to ultraviolet light, and are therefore easier to detect as fakes. But regardless, close inspection reveals that these patches have neither the quality appearance, nor characteristics of period manufacture. Most of the original, post-WWI color insert patches are attributed to the 1920s and 30s. They are well made and show some age even if unused. If a patch looks new, feels new, and is not of quality construction and material, it is probably a fake. Original color insert types are getting fairly scarce - $40.00. The 89th is one of the few examples of shoulder sleeve insignia that were originally subdued (green and black) and transitioned to full color later (1948). *Service:* France, Germany, Czechoslovakia and occupation duty.

90th Infantry Division variations
Left: Standard type with rounded bottom - $5.00 **Middle:** Standard type with more definition around the borders of the red details - $5.00. **Right:** Standard type - $5.00. *Service:* France, Belgium, Germany, Czechoslovakia and occupation duty.

91st Infantry Division variations
Left: Standard type with serrated edges - $5.00. **Middle:** Standard type with flat edges - $5.00 **Right:** Standard type with olive drab border and moderately serrated sides- $15.00.

There is another factory variation with a white border - $40.00, and another with the numbers "91" embroidered in the middle of the tree - $30.00. *Service:* North Africa, Algeria, Italy and occupation duty in Italy and Trieste.

92nd Infantry Division variations

Standard types - $5.00. Note how the different manufacturers leave their mark in the form of, sometimes very subtle, differences in design. The left patch has a small raised border around the buffalo. The patch on the right has more refined tail and rear leg details. Another example exists without the black border around the patch - $40.00. *Service:* North Africa, Italy and occupation duties.

93rd Infantry Division

Standard type - $5.00. *Service:* New Guinea, Solomon Islands, Spice Islands and other island occupations as well as the Philippines.

94th Infantry Division variations

Left: First style, standard type - $5.00. This patch can be found without a black border - $40.00. **Right:** Second style, standard type - $5.00. *Service:* France, Belgium, Luxembourg, Germany and occupation duties.

94ᵗʰ Division variation

An example of a patch that is difficult to find *without* a border. The gray extends all the way to the edge - $45.00

95th Infantry Division variations

The 95th Division is a classic example of how details can vary from manufacturer to manufacturer. All the major fully embroidered factory variations are shown here. **Top left:** First style (1920s-1942), standard type - $20.00. **Top right:** This style is a reproduction of a design utilized during and immediately after WWI. It is cheaply made, embroidered on twill.

These can be found with color inserts between the lower legs of the "K", which signify sub-units within the division. *Middle left:* Standard type, factory variation with no white outline around the "9" and the upper left arm of the "V" passes under the "9" - $10.00. *Middle right:* Same as the previous type except that the upper left arm of the "V" passes *over* the "9" - $10.00. *Bottom left:* Standard type with white outline around the "9" and an olive drab border - $5.00. *Bottom right:* Same as the previous type except that there is no olive drab border - $6.00. *Service:* France, Germany, Holland and occupation duties.

98th Infantry Division variations
Left: This is a scarce factory variation in yellow/gold thread and unusually wide border - $75.00. *Right:* Standard type in the common color $5.00. *Service:* Hawaiian defense.

96th Infantry Division
Standard type- $5.00. Ninety-sixth Division service: Philippines and Okinawa.

98th Infantry Division variation
This example is a unique shade somewhere between the yellow and orange types. Also note the concentrations of thread which create added detail to the eye, and the scar like line running from the upper cheek to the throat - $40.00.

97th Infantry Division
Standard type - $5.00. *Service:* France, Germany, Czechoslovakia, occupation duties in Germany, Philippines, and occupation duties in Japan.

99th Infantry Division variations
Left: Standard type with blue square first - $15.00. *Right:* Standard type with white square first - $5.00. *Service:* France, Belgium, Germany and occupation duties.

100th Infantry Division

Standard type - $5.00. This patch can be found with the number colors reversed (yellow over white) - $40.00. There is also a post-war "AIRBORNE" tab for this patch with matching yellow letters on a matching blue tab. *Service:* France, Germany and occupation duty.

101st Airborne Division

This is a current design, but was advertised on the internet as a WWII piece. The edge is merrowed and the threads are nylon. This patch has a $1.00 value as opposed to the $8.00-$12.00 value of an original. When buying from internet auctions and dealers, check the seller's ratings, ask questions, make sure the seller allows returns (guarantees his/her products), and ask for scans, both front and back if necessary. I never heard from this dealer again. I notified him that this patch was not WWII, and that I wished to return it. That was months ago and I have never received a response. I rated the seller appropriately, and notified the auction host, although there is no real recourse. Numerous variations of the 101st exist. One popular Variation has a white tongue. Most original white tongue types have olive drab "snow" on the reverse rather than the usual white - $50.00+. There are

also numerous head shapes and details. One variant has uncut material between the tab and the patch. The uncut version will have a single stitch of white, yellow and red running downward from the bottom-center of the tab, then a tiny turn to the side, down again, another tiny turn back toward the center, and then down to the center-top of the patch ($50.00). A right facing version can also be found, which is a result of the "combat patch" practice. *Service:* France, Holland, Belgium, Germany and occupation duties.

102nd Infantry Division

Standard type- $6.00. *Service:* France, Germany and occupation duties.

103rd Infantry Division

Standard type - $5.00. Variations exist with six arms on the cactus ($300.00+), and with color inserts horizontally positioned across the bottom of the patch (1920s-1930s). I have heard of one example that has mountains in the background, but I have never seen one. *Service:* France, Germany, Austria and occupation duties.

104th Infantry Division variations
Left: Standard type, but the soldier added red thread to the eye. The meaning is not known, but perhaps the owner was with the division artillery - $6.00. **Right:** Standard type with ribbed weave and highly unusual dark green background - $ 25.00. One factory variation exists with a blue wolf - $20.00. And another with no border $40.00. *Service:* France, Belgium, Germany and occupation duties.

108th Infantry Division (phantom)
This is a standard type - $45.00. A factory variation exists with a much smaller red spike in the center of the mace head. *Service:* Ghost / phantom, Operation Fortitude.

106th Infantry Division
Standard type - $6.00. *Service:* France, Belgium, Germany and occupation duties.

119th Infantry Division (phantom) *variations*
These are standard types with manufacturer variation in flame size - $40.00 each. *Service:* Ghost / phantom, Operation Fortitude.

108th Airborne Division (phantom)
This is a standard type - $45.00. *Service:* Ghost / phantom, Operation Fortitude.

130th Infantry Division (phantom)
This is a standard type - $40.00. *Service:* Ghost / phantom, Operation Fortitude.

135th Airborne Division (phantom)

The 6th and 135th Airborne patches are, by far, the rarest of the standard, fully embroidered, WWII division patches. This is a standard type with matching tab $150.00. This price is substantially higher than the prices you will see for 135th patches offered for sale by dealers or on the internet. This is simply because almost all of the 135th Airborne patches found on the auctions are fakes of varying quality. *Service:* Ghost / phantom, Operation Fortitude.

141st Infantry Division (phantom)
Standard type - $40.00. *Service:* Ghost / phantom, Operation Fortitude.

157th Infantry Division (phantom)
Standard type - $45.00. Variations exist in the dragon details. *Service:* Ghost / Phantom, Operation Fortitude.

Olive drab borders: Many WWII patches can be found with and without an olive drab border. In most cases, the border is a sign of age and quality. Bordered examples are generally worth more. The increase in value for bordered designs can be substantial. The 2nd Infantry Division and 45th Infantry Division are examples of this. Without the border, 2nd or 45th Division patches have a median value of $5.00. With an olive drab border, the 2nd and 45th designs are worth $40.00 - $50.00. The 82nd Airborne patch when found with an olive drab border sells for $800.00+, while the borderless type sells for $10.00. The 77th and 101st experience sharp value increases as well when found with a border. In most cases however, the border will increase the value by $5.00 - $25.00. Division patches that *do not* experience an increase in value when found with the border include: 1st Cav, 3rd ID, 2nd Cav, 7th ID, 14th phantom, 17th phantom, 17th AB, 18th AB, 27th ID, 29th ID, 35th ID, 37th ID, 38th ID, 41st ID, 42nd ID, 48th, 51st, 59th Phantom, 75th ID, 76th ID, 78th ID, 84th ID, 94th ID, 99th ID, 103rd ID, 104th ID, and the 65th Cav. These designs experience a value increase when found *without* an olive drab border.

* Some experts insist that there are no theater made examples of ghost / phantom division patches because these patches never left the States, and were never issued to be worn. I recently viewed a veteran's photographs and noted one that shows at least two soldiers wearing the 17th (ghost/phantom) Division patch. These soldiers are engaged in festive activities, in a cramped English pub, with a mixture of English and British service men and women. The picture is hand dated - May 1944; just prior to the invasion. As part of the deception strategy some ghost / phantom unit patches may have been issued for wear to "corroborate" (in the eyes of Axis intelligence) the existence of these units. This would also suggest that these fresh units were staging for the inevitable invasion. This is the first evidence of the patches actually being worn that I have ever seen. It is possible that some soldiers had English-made variations created. The owner of the photograph said that at least one of the soldiers in the picture was in his (the owner's) "outfit". He has no recollection of ever seeing, receiving, or wearing the patch. The owner was with the 51st Anti-aircraft Artillery Brigade when he arrived in England (before D-Day), and prior to embarking for France, shortly after D-Day. Never say never.....

ARMY DIVISIONAL NICKNAMES

Many divisions were affectionately, and even officially, referred to by nicknames. The nicknames normally have some relationship to the patch design, a divisional specialty, divisional origin, or a significant event associated with the division's history. Many of these divisions were organized initially for WWI. The nicknames they adopted in 1917 and 1918 were largely retained. In fact, several are still used today. Many tabs and scrolls exist that were created both officially and unofficially for wear with divisional insignia. The purpose of this section is to allow the collector to identify separated tabs and associate them with the correct patch. This is also interesting information to include on cards or labels that are displayed with patches. Additionally, many publications and articles mention divisions by nickname alone. This is particularly true of WWII period publications. Therefore, should the need arise to positively identify what division is being referred to, the reader can consult this list for confirmation. In the event that more than one nickname was associated with a division, all will be listed.

* Armored Division nicknames are listed in the Armored Division section.

Note: Most of these nicknames are very well known. Others have been noted in period publications, documents, and letters. A few like "Pacific Fire", which is listed with the 41st Division, surfaced in period letters from different WWII, 41st Division veterans. Even though its use may have been on a very limited scale, it may be of interest to historians. More importantly for a collector, it could have found its way onto an unofficial tab or patch adopted by a unit in the field. Hence their mention here may provide a helpful lead to a collector who finds one.

ARMY DIVISIONS

		Fourth Division	*"Ivy"*
First Division	*"Big Red One"* - *"Fighting First"* This is probably the most recognized American division patch.	**Fifth Division**	*"Red Diamond"*
		Sixth Division	*"Red Star"* - *"Sight Seeing Sixth"*
First Cavalry Division	*"First Team"* - *"Hell For Leather"*	**Seventh Division**	*"Hourglass"* - *"Sight Seeing Seventh"*
Second Division	*"Indian Head"*	**Eighth Division**	*"Pathfinder"* - *"Golden Arrow"*
Third Division	*"Rock of the Marne"* -*"Marne"*		

Ninth Division	"Varsity" - "Old Reliable"	**Forty-first Division**	"Sunset" - "Pacific Fire" - "Jungaleer"
Tenth Division	"Mountaineer"	**Forty-second Division**	"Rainbow"
Eleventh Division	"Angels"	**Forty-third Division**	"Winged Victory" - "Red Wing"
Twelfth Division	"Philippine"		
Seventeenth Division	"Golden Talon" - "Thunder From Heaven"	**Forty-fifth Division**	"Thunderbird"
Twenty-third Division	"American" This was also the unit designation during WW II. It wasn't until 1954, that the patch was authorized for wear by the Twenty-third Infantry Division.	**Sixty-third Division**	"Blood And Fire"
		Sixty-fifth Division	"Battle-Axe" - "Halberdiers"
		Sixty-sixth Division	"Black Panther" – "Mad Cat"
		Sixty-ninth Division	"Fighting Sixty-ninth"
Twenty-fourth Division	"Victory" Prior to 1941, the official designation of this unit was "The Hawaiian Division".	**Seventieth Division**	"Trailblazer"
		Seventy-first Division	"Red Circle"
		Seventy-sixth Division	"Onoway" - "Liberty Bell"
Twenty-fifth Division	"Tropic Lightning" - "Pineapple"	**Seventy-seventh Division**	"Statue of Liberty" - "Metropolitan"
Twenty-sixth Division	"Yankee"	**Seventy-eighth Division**	"Lightning"
Twenty-seventh Division	"New York" - "Empire"	**Seventy-ninth Division**	"Lorraine" - "Cross of Lorraine"
Twenty-eighth Division	"Keystone" - "Pennsylvania"		
Twenty-ninth Division	"Blue and Gray"		
Thirtieth Division	"Old Hickory"	**Eightieth Division**	"Blue Ridge"
Thirty-first Division	"Dixie"	**Eighty-first Division**	"Wildcat" - Stonewall Jackson" - "Bob Cat"
Thirty-second Division	"Red Arrow" - "Iron Jaw" - "Terrible"	**Eighty-second Division**	"All American" (Airborne tab added in 1942)
Thirty-third Division	"Illinois" - "Prairie"		
Thirty-fourth Division	"Red Bull" - "Sandstorm"	**Eighty-third Division**	"Thunderbolt" - "Ohio"
Thirty-fifth Division	"Santa Fe"	**Eighty-fourth Division**	"Railsplitters" - "Lincoln"
Thirty-sixth Division	"Texas" - "Lone Star" - "Panther"	**Eighty-fifth Division**	"Custer"
		Eighty-sixth Division	"Black Hawk"
Thirty-seventh Division	"Buckeye"	**Eighty-seventh Division**	"Golden Acorn"
Thirty-eighth Division	"Cyclone"	**Eighty-eighth Division**	"Blue Devil" - "Cloverleaf"
Thirty-ninth Division WWII	"Delta" not active during	**Eighty-ninth Division**	"Rolling W" - "Middle West"
Fortieth Division	"Fire in the Sky" - "Blazing Star" - "Sunshine" - "Rattlesnake"	**Nintieth Division**	"Tough Ombres" - "Texas Oklahoma" - "Alamo"

Ninety-first Division	*"Wild West" - "Powder River"*	**Ninety-ninth Division**	*"Checkerboard"*
Ninety-second Division	*"Buffalo"*	**One-hundredth Division**	*"Century"*
Ninety-fourth Division	*"Neuf Cats" - "Neuf Quatres"*	**One-hundred and first Division**	*"Screaming Eagles"* (Airborne tab added in 1942)
Ninety-fifth Division	*"Victory" - "OK"*	**One-hundred and second Division**	*"Ozark"*
Ninety-sixth Division	*"Deadeye"*	**One-hundred and third Division**	*"Cactus"*
Ninety-seventh Division	*"Trident"*	**One-hundred and fourth Division**	*"Timber Wolf"*
Ninety-eighth Division	*"Iroquois"*	**One-hundred and sixth Division**	*"Golden Lion"*

ARMORED DIVISIONS & RELATED UNITS

All standard issue armored division patches utilized the same design. Only the Arabic numeral designating the division number changed. During the war, many units adopted identical designs with their respective unit identifier displayed. Some used letters or combinations to denote groups, regiments, battalions, companies, headquarters, and independent units. The Armored Force patch (also known as Armored Center or Armored Command) is the same design except that no identifying numbers or letters are displayed in the yellow field. Many collectors believe that the Armored Force patch was worn exclusively by stateside personnel assigned to the Armored Center. Actually, thousands of armored troops assigned to independent units wore the Armored Force patch in the field. In fact, most of the original patches bearing battalion or other sub-divisional identifications are Armored Force patches that the owner applied the numbers / letters to, or had them applied locally. Thousands of these patches were modified by the addition of numbers and letters in Germany, during the occupation. Almost all U.S. factory embroidered, battalion numbered examples are immediate post-war patches made as souvenirs for the GIs returning home. Regardless, they are still period patches and are of interest to collectors. The number of different units is impossible to assess. The battalion types run into the "900"s, and probably beyond, although many of these are Korean vintage, wrongly represented as WWII. For obvious reasons, I have opted to show representative examples rather than illustrate hundreds of patches almost identical in design and detail. WWII armored patches all had olive drab borders. When the army adopted the new army green uniform color, the border color of armored patches changed as well. Therefore, when you see armor patches with dark (army green) borders, they are post-1958 manufacture.

759th Light Tank Battalion patch

This is a standard type that was made as a souvenir for returning veterans in the 1940s - $10.00. Battalion types have a higher market value than the more commonly encountered and plentiful division types. Collectors should beware that the market is literally flooded with reproduction armored unit patches that are extremely well made. Signs of age, use and heavy snow on the reverse are about the only methods of identifying period examples. Another characteristic of WWII armored patches is that many were about 1/4 smaller than the patches worn today.

Bevo 526th Armored Infantry Battalion patch and tab

526th Armored Infantry Battalion patch in reverse

Very few WWII patches are genuine bevo types, although many patches are erroneously labeled as such. This is a true German bevo weave patch. By examining the front and reverse, you can see the very distinctive characteristics of a bevo design. The bevo 526th is a scarce and desirable patch - $125.00. The correct "BATTLEAXE" tab is also bevo and equally valuable - $75.00. The tab shown was represented as original by a very well known and reputable dealer. The tab is actually a reproduction with nylon embroidery on wool. This is an example of a recognized expert being fooled. Upon inspection, the tab felt stiff and new. When an ultraviolet light was passed over the reverse side of the tab, white threads glowed brilliantly indicating the white thread was nylon, and consequently, post-WWII. *Service:* The 526th has a very interesting history. The unit arrived in England and began training with "GIZMOS". These were Sherman tanks mounting brilliant spotlights that emitted a purple light instead of the gun. They were intended to blind the enemy, but the 526th never operated with them in combat. After disembarking on Utah Beach in France, in August 1944, the 526th worked its way to Belgium, and

played a role during the Battle of the Bulge. Eventually, the unit began operating as a tactical force for the 6860th Headquarters Detachment, known as T-Force. T-Force worked in concert with the Office of Strategic Services (OSS) and was tasked with intelligence and counter intelligence operations. As the American forces advanced into Germany, T-Force would identify targets of extreme strategic importance, civilian or military. The 526th's responsibility was to infiltrate those targets, seize them intact if possible, and hold them until relieved by advancing forces. Targets included Gestapo offices, factories, headquarters facilities, locations of significant historical / cultural importance, and so on. The 526th was considered an elite unit with highly classified responsibilities.

Armored Divisions were organized to provide mobile, big gun, deep penetration capability. The intent was to use them as relatively self-sufficient combat teams that could breech enemy lines. They were expected to exploit successes through the use of their own organic assets including infantry, engineers, and artillery. Division compositions varied due to tactical considerations, and the highly inconsistent methods of the commanders who directed them.

There were twenty armored division patches manufactured during WWII, numbered 1 - 20. Only sixteen of those were active during WWII, but patches were made for the others in anticipation that they would be activated prior to the war's end. The 15th, 17th, 19th and 20th Armored Divisions were not activated.

Like their infantry counterparts, armored divisions acquired nicknames during their war time service. Many reference books and publications of the period refer to these units by their nicknames. As a result of this, tabs can be found that were unofficially adopted for wear underneath the division patches, and bear the divisional nicknames. Because the tabs are commonly found separately, I have listed each division with its respective nickname to assist collectors in associating the tabs with their respective patch.

1st Armored -	*"OLD IRONSIDES"*
2nd Armored -	*"HELL ON WHEELS"*
3rd Armored -	*"SPEARHEAD"*
4th Armored -	*"BREAKTHROUGH"*
5th Armored -	*"VICTORY"*
6th Armored -	*"SUPER SIXTH"*
7th Armored -	*"THE LUCKY SEVENTH"*
8th Armored -	*"THUNDERING HERD"*
	– *" IRON DUCE"*
	– *"IRON SNAKE"*
9th Armored -	*"REMAGEN"* – *"PHANTOM"*
10th Armored -	*"TIGER"*
11th Armored -	*"THUNDERBOLT"*
12th Armored -	*"HELLCAT"* – *" SPEED IS THE PASS WORD"*
13th Armored -	*"BLACK CAT"*
14th Armored -	*"LIBERATORS"*

Example of an Armored Division tab for the 1st Armored Division.

Many WWII vintage armored patches were smaller than current designs. Consequently, the tabs are often times smaller then their current counterparts. Tabs can be found in a multitude of colors. Original embroidered tabs may vary from $5.00 - $40.00.

3rd Armored Division

This is a standard type with unusually bright shade of yellow - $10.00.

Armored Division service: To minimize redundancy only two representative armored division patches are shown (3rd and 20th). However, I have listed the WWII service locations for each active armored division below:

1st Armored Division Ireland, North Africa, Italy.

2nd Armored Division North Africa, Sicily, France, Belgium, Germany.

3rd Armored Division England, France, Belgium, Germany.

4th Armored Division England, France, Belgium, Germany.

5th Armored Division England, France, Belgium, Germany.

6th Armored Division England, France, Germany.

7th Armored Division England, France, Belgium, Germany.

8th Armored Division Served as a training unit in the states prior to embarking for Europe. England, France, Holland, Germany.

9th Armored Division England, France, Belgium, Germany, Czechoslovakia.

10th Armored Division France, Belgium, Germany, Austria.

11th Armored Division England, France, Belgium, Germany, Austria

12th Armored Division England, France, Germany, Austria

13th Armored Division France, Germany, Austria.

14th Armored Division France, Belgium, Germany

16th Armored Division France, Germany, Czechoslovakia.

20th Armored Division France, Belgium, Germany, Austria.

20th Armored Division patch

This patch is an example of the comparatively small size of many 1940s armored types. Many WWII armored patches measure roughly 3-1/4" tall and wide, while most current types are approximately 4" tall and wide. This is a standard type - $6.00.

Green back armored division patch

Like other WWII patches, the armored designs can be found with green backs as well.

Green back types are not scarce, but they are frequently being marketed as such by enterprising vendors. Some collectors may pay more, but there is no factual justification for any appreciable difference in value.

1st Armored Division proficiency patch

This patch was awarded and worn unofficially by personnel of the 1st Armored Division. The badge signified an extraordinary degree of competence, similar to an Expert Infantryman's Badge (EIB) - $25.00.

Embroidered on felt jacket patch for Armored Forces

This patch was a souvenir patch that could be purchased at the post exchange. These larger designs were normally worn on the back of a jacket. Every branch had similar patches - $15.00.

Airborne Armored Detachment

As allied forces tightened the stranglehold on Japan, plans were underway for an invasion of the Japanese mainland. Those plans included an airborne armored element. Although the surrender rendered the invasion unnecessary, this patch configuration was worn by members of the provisional unit's cadre. An original uniform with this patch configuration is extremely rare. Obviously, it can be easily reproduced by combining two very common insignias. Therefore, without photographs or documents corroborating association with this unit, the patch combination has no real value. I am unaware of any one-piece, overseas-made examples. However the possibility is quite strong that one-piece examples exist. I would estimate the value of an original, one-piece, theater-made airborne armor patch to be $500.00+.

The Armored School

This patch was the first design adopted for wear by Armored School personnel. This patch is getting fairly difficult to find - $40.00.

Armored Demonstration Regiment

This is a standard type - $45.00. The Demonstration Regiment was composed of a select cadre of armored personnel. It was responsible for advanced, specialized training.

The Armored School

This patch was worn by Armored School personnel in lieu of the earlier "S" design shown previously. The tab was worn below a standard Armored Force Headquarters patch. Both the patch and tab are fully embroidered - $15.00.

———◦◦◦———

Variations of the Tank Destroyer Forces patch

Due to the complex details of the Tank Destroyer patch, each manufacturer produced a slightly different rendition. Only a few of the myriad types are illustrated here. Differences can be found in the tongue, eyes, nose, teeth, shape of the head, whiskers, ears and every other detail. Note the patch shown (center) where the eyes were omitted completely. I have seen another example with no teeth. Some types have the gun pointing to the left and another has a gun on both sides. The left

pointing gun is a scarce type - $125.00. The two gun type is even more scarce - $400.00. Originally, the patch was produced in an 8-wheel configuration ($12.00). It was later decided that the track and wheel detail was too complex. The design was subsequently changed to a 4-wheel configuration with reduced track detail - $6.00. One manufacturer produced a 6-wheel design, which is very rare - $300.00. *Service:* Tank Destroyer units served with distinction in every theater.

Advertisement from a wartime LIFE *Magazine*

Oversize Italian made Tank Destroyer patch.

Beautifully executed Italian design. It is hand embroidered with silk threads in a typical swirl and loop fashion. The patch measures some 5 inches across and was directly applied to the breast of a field jacket. Similar designs in a smaller size were embroidered on scarves and sold to GIs for their sweetheart back home. This example - $175.00.

In mid-1999, I purchased a Tank Destroyer patch from an internet auction that was embroidered on twill. Having never seen a twill variation before, I inquired further. The vendor had a "bought it from the vet story", and I finally decided to bid, and won. Upon inspection it was instantly obvious that the patch was a brand new, poor quality reproduction. It may have been a souvenir item for reunions. In any case, I had paid $125.00. After some debate with the vendor he refunded my money. I probably return three patches for every ten I buy, and that's after soliciting additional photos and information before I purchase. The prices of patches are climbing faster than I can update the prices in this book. I have spent $1000.00 for particularly rare pieces. Before you buy a patch, any patch, make sure the dealer offers an inspection period and money back guarantee. Any dealer who sells quality material will be delighted to back his/her product. If you don't take this advice, I *absolutely guarantee* that you are in for a dreadfully expensive education.

MISCELLANEOUS COMBAT UNITS

Filipino Battalions

Standard type with green "snow" on the reverse - $15.00. Variations in size and examples with embroidered details on yellow felt are relatively common. *Service:* assisted in the liberation of the Philippines and the Island of Samar, near Leyte. The Fillipino Battalions were part of the 1st Filipino Regiment.

56th Cavalry Brigade.

Embroidered on wool - $20.00. *Service:* This unit was dismounted and dispersed in 1940. It did not see service as a unit during WWII.

3rd Armored Cavalry regiment

German made, embroidered on felt - $45.00. Note the light mothing in the green felt at upper-left. This patch design was personally approved by General Patton in 1944. *Service:* Northern France, Rhineland, Ardennes-Alsace.

5307th Composite Unit (Merrill's Marauders).

This is one of two commonly encountered Merrill's Marauders patch designs. It is a standard type - $50.00.

5307th Composite Unit (Merrill's Marauders).

Left: Air Medal with inscription on the reverse side. **Middle bottom:** Sterling silver lapel pin for OSS veterans. **Right:** The second commonly encountered style of the Merrill's Marauders patch - $75.00. This group of items belonged to a man who served with Merrill's Marauders and Detachment 101, of the Office of Strategic Services (OSS). *Service:* Organized in the China, Burma, India Theater in 1943, and operated in Northern Burma. The Marauders served as long range combat patrols and assisted in clearing the Japanese from the path the Ledo Road would take. These were the forerunners of today's Long Range Recon Patrols (LRRPs). A few members of the small group that survived and were fit enough to continue service, became members of a unit known as "Mars Force", often times referred to as The "Mars Task Force". This new unit adopted essentially the same patch design without displaying the words "Merrills Marauders". As with any other patch worn in the China, Burma, India Theater, these patches exist in myriad variations including embroidered, silk, bullion, leather and printed types.

trim around the edge. This piece was hand-embroidered on a coarse blue twill $250.00. The Mars Task Force patch design was continued from the disbanded Merrill's Marauders patch. This same design has endured and is now the basic insignia of the United States Army Rangers.

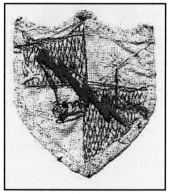

Mars Task Force patch in reverse

This shows the reverse side of the Mars Task Force patch. Each hand-embroidered type is literally one of a kind. But in a general sense, the appearance of this patch is pretty typical of pieces originating from the China, Burma, India Theater.

Close-up of the OSS veteran's pin.

The Office of Strategic Services (OSS) was the forerunner of American Special Forces. The OSS dispatched personnel all over the world to gather intelligence, conduct "black operations" (assassination, sabotage, espionage and the like), and to operate behind enemy lines in concert with native guerrillas. One of the most famous and successful operational OSS units was Detachment 101. With its headquarters in New Delhi, India, 101's primary responsibility was to organize, train and lead native bands against Japanese forces in Burma. These bands consisted primarily of natives known as Jingpaws, or Kachins. This concept of insurgent warfare nurtured by the OSS, would be seen again when Special Forces troopers achieved extraordinary successes with natives in Vietnam, China, Cambodia, and Laos.

Mars Task Force.

This is a Mars Task Force patch originating from India. The green sections are woven in a classic Indian style and the sun and star are in silver bullion. There is also bullion

Reverse side of the Air Medal

This medal is named to its recipient: "CPL. ROB-ERT A. DALTON DET 101 OSS BURMA". This soldier's group also includes a large leather China, Burma, India patch for wear on the back of a jacket, and a named Good Conduct Medal. OSS related items are ultra rare. Attributed groups like this are very desirable - $1500.00.

bottom. It is believed that these patches were not worn in combat, but rather were produced for Americans as souvenirs of their service, and for the natives as gifts in recognition of their contribution to the war effort.. *Service:* The Kachins/(Jingpaws were recruited and trained by members of OSS Detachment 101 and fought as guerrillas in support of allied forces in Burma.

4th Ranger Battalion

This is an example of the scroll type patch worn by Ranger Battalions - $25.00. Six battalions were activated during WWII, although scrolls exist with battalion numbers 1-9. All the scroll patches were identical except for the battalion number. Therefore, to avoid redundancy only the 4th Battalion scroll is illustrated as a representative example. The Ranger scrolls are one of the most reproduced sets of WWII cloth insignia. Originals and reproductions alike are embroidered on black wool. Most have a cheesecloth backing. Many of the reproductions utilize white nylon threads and they can be detected with ultraviolet light. Others do not. Look for age, quality workmanship, signs of wear, and other clues that might help you make a sound decision.

1st Battalion service: North Africa, Sicily, Italy.

2nd Battalion service: England, France, Belgium, Luxembourg, Germany, Czechoslovakia and occupation duties.

3rd Battalion service: North Africa, Sicily, Italy.

4th Battalion service: North Africa, Sicily, Italy. Many of this battalion's personnel helped to form the cadre of the 1st Special Service Force.

5th Battalion service: England, France, Germany

6th Battalion service: (Formerly the 98th Field Artillery Battalion) New Guinea, Philippines, occupation duties in Japan.

7th, 8th and 9th Battalion service: Not active.

Jingpaw Rangers and Kachin Rangers

U.S. fully embroidered type - $80.00. "Jingpaw" was the tribal name of the Kachins. The GIs used the terms interchangeably and so both found their way onto the patch. Many of these patches were modified in the field by natives. The blue section was cut off. The red and white section was turned upside down, with the point facing upward. The strip with "USA" was cut off completely, and the remaining section with "Jingpaw Rangers" or "Kachin Rangers" was re-applied across the base of the upside down shield. Bullion, silk and various other theater made examples can be found. This patch was also factory made in an inverted configuration with the pointed end at top, and the unit name in a blue banner across the

Ranger Battalion patch

This patch was intended for wear by all Ranger Battalions - $35.00. I have seen this patch worn on the right, left, or both shoulders. This is another example of a patch who's value has been suddenly and temporarily, affected by the movie *Saving Private Ryan*. A reasonable market value is $35.00. In a post-movie frenzy, this patch was selling for double its value. The prices have since returned to normal.

98th Field Artillery Battalion

This patch is embroidered on wool. Note the moderate moth damage near the nose - $35.00. *Service:* Australia, New Guinea. This battalion became the 6th Ranger Battalion in 1944.

Allied Task Force 9 (Kiska Task Force) variations

Left: Standard type in dark blue - $20.00 ***Right:*** Printed on canvas. This variation is attributed to members of the 1st Special Service Force who participated in the invasion of Kiska - $50.00. This is one of the few American shoulder sleeve patches that was commonly worn on both sleeves. **ATF-9 service:** Invasion of Kiska.

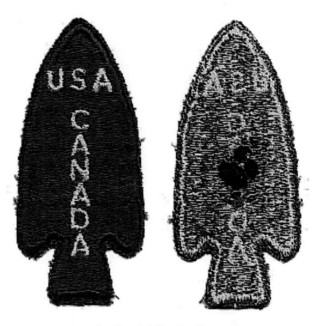

1st Special Service Force

Standard type - $75.00. Note the olive drab cut-edge. Also note the snow on the reverse side. This is what an original 1st SSF, fully embroidered patch should look like. There is some glue and paper residue on the back from a previous display. This sort of glue residue does not adversely effect the value of scarcer patches like this one. As long as there is no damage to the front, the value is retained. Collectors should find display options however, that do not cause damage or staining of any kind. *Service:* Commonly known as the "Devil's Brigade", the 1st SSF was a combined Canadian/American special operations force. 1st SSF personnel were trained to perform commando type missions, and received extensive winter warfare/mountain training. This unit participated in the unopposed invasion of Kiska, in the Aleutians. Soon after, the 1st SSF proceeded to Italy, via North Africa, where the brigade fought in a number of violent engagements including the battle at Anzio. The 1st SSF was then assigned to the 1st Airborne Task Force and landed in France. After extensive combat the 1st SSF was disbanded. There is a lineage associating the 1st SSF (including Rangers), the 99th Infantry Battalion, and the 474th Regiment (later the 74th Regimental Combat Team). This association is suggested by the common details found in the patches of all three units.

99th Infantry Battalion

Standard type - $15.00. Another variation exists with an olive drab border - $50.00. *Service:* England, France, Belgium, Germany. This unit was de-activated and its personnel transferred to the 474th Infantry Regiment.

2nd Airborne Infantry Brigade

This is a standard type with separate tab - $20.00. *Service:* Ireland, France, Germany.

474th Infantry Regiment (Error) and 474th Infantry Regiment (correct)

This is a standard type, but blue was used as the background rather than the prescribed red - $15.00. For the red type - $10.00. *Service:* (This unit consisted of ex-Rangers, 1st Special Service Force men, and 99th Infantry Battalion personnel). France, Germany, occupation duties, Norway. This unit became the 74th Regimental Combat Team.

442nd Combat Team (2nd style) and 442nd Combat team (1st style)

Standard, second style - $20.00. *Service:* Italy, France, inactivated in the pacific. This unit was composed of Japanese Americans.

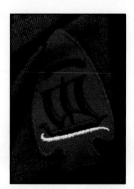

474th Regiment variation

German-made, embroidered on red twill - $35.00. The red arrowhead background of the 474th is a tribute to the many members who served previously with the 1st SSF. The black scroll at top symbolizes members with prior Ranger service. The viking ship is in recognition of members formerly serving with the 99th Infantry Battalion.

Examples of WWII Airborne insignia

patches exist with different materials, sizes and colors. **504th PIR** *service:* (82nd Airborne Division), Sicily, Italy, France, Germany, Belgium. Paratroopers and glider infantrymen served in every theater.

187th Paraglider Infantry (PGI) variations

Note: Much like smaller Air Force units, airborne units adopted many unofficial patches during WWII. A large proportion are theater-made. The number of unofficial designs is staggering, and there is simply not room in this book to illustrate them. Therefore, I have included a couple representative airborne unit patches to serve as examples. *Top left:* Parachute artillery cap patch, embroidered on twill - $20.00. *Top right:* Parachute infantry cap patch, embroidered on blue felt - $15.00. *Middle:* Pocket patch of the 504th Parachute Infantry Regiment (PIR), hand-embroidered on light gray wool. This patch was probably made in Italy - $500.00. *Bottom left:* Paraglider Infantry cap patch for enlisted men (left facing). This is a fully embroidered Japanese made example and an interesting variation. Note the added detail of a glass blister on the top of the glider, just aft of the cockpit, and a more rounded, refined nose - $25.00. *Bottom middle:* Airborne artillery parachute wings and oval. The wings are embroidered on a solid red cotton base - $30.00. *Bottom right:* Paraglider Infantryman cap patch for officers (Right facing). This is a fully embroidered theater-made example - $12.00. A patch was also manufactured for troops that were strictly gliderborne. These are discs, in red and blue like the parachute types, but with a white glider instead of a parachute. Later in the war, the paraglider cap patch was adopted for simplification and eliminated the numerous earlier styles. The right and left facing paraglider patches were intended to differentiate officers and enlisted men. The patch was supposed to be worn with the glider facing the front. Enlisted wore theirs on the left side of the cap, and officers on the right side. Period photographs show however, that all ranks utilized whatever was available. The patch can be found on the wrong side of the cap, and I have also seen the patch being worn with the glider facing rearward. In excess of sixty-five variations of the cap

Top: This example was produced in the Philippines, and is painted on leather. If you look closely, you can see the "Devil Dog's" eyes, and tongue licking his chops. "187" appears on the dog's neck and a small glider appears near the bottom. The remnants of what was once a parachute canopy can be seen behind the dog's head. The leather patch was then sewn onto a leather jacket owned by Leo Quirino, 187th PGI, 11th Airborne Division. Airborne troops in the pacific and European areas acquired an affection for leather flight jackets. This patch was applied to a G-1 flight jacket, which was a type issued by the Navy and Marine Corps. The 187th served with the 11th Airborne Division in the pacific, where the G-1 jacket was readily available. Army Air Force jackets, like the A-2, were more prevalent in Europe. The creator has taken some artistic license and altered the colors and details of the 187th patch. This may have been a whim, or it may have been a matter of necessity based upon whatever paints were available. **Bottom:** This is the standard patch for the 187th Paraglider Infantry Regiment - $125.00. *Service:* The 187th PGI served with the 11th Airborne Division. Members saw action in New Guinea, the Philippines and occupation duties in Japan.

Unofficial sub-unit insignia of the 187th PGI Regiment

This is another Philippine made, hand painted leather patch. "187" is visible to the left of the shroud lines, and "P/G INF" is visible to the right. At top is "DEVILS FROM HEAVEN". At the bottom is the 11th Airborne Division design. The gorilla is wearing an overseas cap with a distinctive insignia on it. This may have been a design adopted by one of the regiment's battalions or companies.

Patch distribution on the front of the 187th Paraglider jacket

Back of the 187th Paraglider jacket

This is the back of the jacket showing a large patch with a cartoon paratrooper drifting through clouds and snow capped peaks. "DEVILS FROM HEAVEN" is painted above and below the picture. $1500.00

Another hand painted Airborne leather patch

The top patch has U.S. Parachute wings with " 11TH AIRBORNE" at top. The lower patch has "LEO QUIRINO 187 P/G INF U.S. PARATROOPS".

Army Amphibian Units

Standard type - $7.00. *Service:* Consisted of several brigades, which served in the European and Pacific Theaters. These troops were at the forefront of every significant amphibious assault that occurred throughout the war.

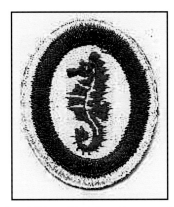

Amphibious Training Command
(Engineer Special Brigades was a post-war designation for this insignia)

Standard type - $5.00. Another fairly common variation does not have the outer white border and the blue extends to the edges. This is one of the few patches authorized to be worn on the pocket. Tabs were made to accompany this patch. The tabs are small and are normally found with orange/red letters or numbers embroidered on a white arc. Examples include "SECOND", "FIFTH" and "498TH". These titles represent the wearer's respective brigade number. As far as I have been able to determine, these tabs are post-war and were not worn during WWII. *Service:* This unit was responsible for training army amphibious units. Interestingly, because of the engineer's history of operating small watercraft in freshwater and inland environments, they were selected to fulfill this role.

36th Engineer Combat Regiment

This is a French-made example, fully embroidered with a wave pattern weave - $20.00. *Service:* The 36th was assigned to the Atlantic Amphibious Corps and landed in French Morocco in 1942, minus one battalion, which landed in Algiers. The 36th proceeded to Sicily, participating in that invasion and eventually took part in the invasion of Italy. After fighting on the beaches the 36th became involved in the bloody confrontation at Anzio. The regiment found itself in the middle of yet another invasion and landed in Southern France in August 1944, and fought its way into Germany. Amongst other things, the 36th fought as infantry, built bridges, managed ports, cleared beaches, and supervised the movement of supplies. This regiment was credited with five amphibious assaults and ten campaigns. The patch worn by the 36th, was an unofficial design authorized for local wear. The patch was worn on the pocket.

1778th Combat Engineers

Embroidered on felt with cheesecloth backing - $25.00. This patch was authorized in Europe for local wear only.

1778th Engineers in reverse, showing the fine-cheesecloth backing

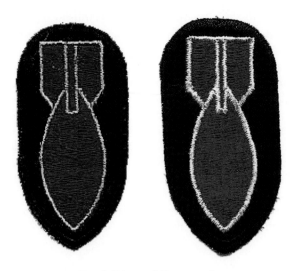

Bomb Disposal Personnel

Left: Standard type - $8.00. **Right:** White outline variation, which is more difficult to find - $20.00. This patch was worn by all bomb disposal personnel including training and operational units. It was worn on the pocket of a shirt or on the lower sleeve of a coat. Some variations have a white outline around the bomb.

Red Ball Express

This patch was French made and is usually embroidered on a mustard colored twill. Some have periods after the letters and others, like this one, do not. The patch is scarce - $75.00. In 1999, a number of Red Ball Express patches began surfacing and became fairly common place on internet auctions. They are very, very well made reproductions. Unless you know the provenance of the patch, it is almost impossible to differentiate between originals and these high quality reproductions. When a rare patch surfaces on the internet, spend some time searching other dealer's inventories as well. If several examples of a rare patch surface at the same time on various sites, the collector should be very cautious. Reproductions are usually produced in batches and they will appear for sale at several places almost simultaneously. *Service:* After the landings in France, and due to the shortage of operational port facilities, it became necessary to truck supplies from the beaches to the front lines. This route became quite extended before the logistics problems were improved. The officers and men involved in that vital supply mission adopted this unofficial design for local wear. The "T C" represents Transportation Corps. The "M T S" stands for "Motorized Transport Service". Personnel wore these on their caps as well as their sleeves.

Bomb Disposal specialist amidst German aircraft wreckage

This soldier maintains a happy-go-lucky attitude despite the dangerousness of his work. This photo was taken in France, 1945.

Invasion brassard

The Invasion Flag was worn by personnel of all services who were participating in an assault. One purpose was to prevent casualties due to misidentification during landings such as those in Sicily, Italy, France and Holland. Additionally, The allies anticipated extensive efforts at retribution directed at Axis troops by the local populations once the arrival of the Allies was known, or immediately imminent. Revenge crazed locals may easily mistake an allied soldier for a German. In the case of the landings in North Africa, it was hoped that Vichy French forces would be reluctant to fire on American troops coming ashore. Airborne forces that were dropped behind enemy lines wore these identification flags as well. Parachute troops not only found themselves in places where the locals expected only Axis troops to be, but they were also in front of friendly ground troops. In most cases they were expected to "link-up" with advancing friendly formations and frequently operated at night. A dangerous proposition in the best of circumstances. The flag was just a little added insurance that these link-ups did not result in tragic confrontations. The invasion flags could be sewn on the sleeve, affixed to the helmet, or like the one pictured here, were made to be worn like a brassard. This particular piece can be laced up for a snug fit, and worn on the sleeve. It is printed on oilcloth - $50.00.

solely of interwoven threads with no base material. Although they look like cut-edge patches from a distance, close examination of the edges (magnifying glass) will reveal cut thread-ends all the way around. The patch is so rare that there is really no market reference. I know of one that sold for $1600.00 ten years ago. In 2002 a bullion example and badly damaged embroidered type sold as a set for $700.00 and immediately thereafter, I was offered $2200.00 for the specimen shown here. A realistic range might be $1,200.00-$1,600.00

A bullion example of the 6860th HQ Detachment (T-Force) patch

This is arguably the Holy Grail of WWII fully embroidered patches. This unit consisted of approximately 160 men, who were responsible for gathering intelligence in preparation for the invasion of Southern France. In 1944, prior to the T-Force designation, these officers and men worked for Allied Forces HQ and supported the U.S. Seventh and French 1st Armies. Consequently, this patch incorporates elements from the patches of the six units mentioned. Shortly after the invasion of Southern France, the unit was disbanded. Some members had these patches produced in France, and they were worn unofficially until the members were re-assigned. Note the vertical row-weave. Most originals consist

MISCELLANEOUS

Official War Correspondent

Embroidered on twill with mesh backing - $20.00. Many variations in this patch exist with different shapes, sizes, colors, and materials. *Service:* Hundreds of war correspondents were deployed by the military in every theater of operations. Their objective was to keep the American people appraised of American war efforts from a first-hand perspective. Unlike today, reports were often flowery and optimistic regardless of the facts. This was done to bolster the spirits of the American people and ensure a continuing national commitment.

Auxillary Military Police

Standard type, embroidered on twill - $10.00. Note that some of the "L" in POLICE, has come off. Many variations in color and shape exist as they were often produced at the request of individual plants or facilities. *Service:* The Auxillary Military Police were organized to act as security at locations of military value. Ship building yards, ports, factories, and other facilities. AMP training was coordinated by the Service Command with jurisdiction, but AMP personnel were supervised at the local level.

Yank Magazine Correspondent

Embroidered on twill - $50.00. This patch was worn by correspondents assigned to the YANK military magazine staff. YANK had field offices all over the world and tailored it's magazine to the GI readership.

Civilian in Uniform

Standard type, embroidered on twill - $4.00. Also found in white and black. This particular patch was worn on the collar. Variations of this patch can be found with foreign location names across the top, above the "US". Yet another variation indicates that the wearer can speak a second language. For example "RUSSIAN" may appear above the "US". For these fairly scarce variations - $35.00+. There are many variations of this insignia, as well as a set of square patches in the same material, which indicate the wearer's specific function. These square patches include: Technical Representative, Messenger, Automotive Advisor, Chauffer, Analyst, Photographer, Radio Commentator, Scientific Consultant, Correpondent, Observor, and more. Uniform requirements varied depending on the duties being performed, but when the uniform was required, it was identical to a military uniform with these patches applied. *Service:* There were many civilians who worked closely with the military, both home and overseas. Occasionally, a civilian may be required to perform their duties in harm's way. Although extremely infrequent, an example may include a factory representative from an aircraft manufacturer finding it necessary to accompany a plane under combat conditions. The uniform was necessary to insure proper treatment in the event that the aircraft was downed and the civilian captured. If the worker was captured in civilian attire, they could technically be shot as a spy.

Manhattan District project

Standard type - $15.00. *Service:* This project involved gathering the resources, conducting the research, and actually building the atomic bomb. The patch was authorized for wear by military personnel assigned to the project.

Significant Headquarters & Commands

During WWII the United States dispatched her Armed Forces to all corners of the globe. This created an enormously complicated system of logistics, command and control. Organizations were created in every theater to assist with administration, training, construction, transportation, medical affairs, maintenance, supply, and the actual execution of offensive and defensive activities. Each theater of operation had a headquarters and their own distinctive patch. In addition to those, thousands of troops were assigned to defense and base commands. Defense commands were responsible for the defense of U.S. Territories. Base commands served the same defensive role in areas outside U.S. territory. The London Base Command is an exception. This organization was involved with service and supply activities. It was not engaged in active defense of the United States. A patch exists for each base and defense command. The other patches in this section were worn by personnel assigned to various headquarters, training commands, and other vital military organizations. Most of the major headquarters and commands established during WWII, which were authorized to wear or known to wear a cloth shoulder insignia are included here.

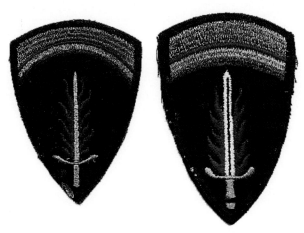

Supreme Headquarters Allied Expeditionary Forces
(wartime)

Left: Standard type in smaller size - $10.00. **Right:** Standard type but larger - $10.00. SHAEF was a multinational command under the leadership of General Dwight D. Eisenhower. It's mission was to destroy the Axis forces on the European Continent. The wartime SHAEF patch has a black field.

U.S. Army Headquarters Europe

Left: Standard type with Berlin tab - $8.00 **Right:** German-made example in a bevo-like weave - $6.00. The U.S. Army Headquarters Europe patch is identical to the wartime design except that the black sky (symbolizing Axis oppression over Europe) is now blue. This design was approved when the Axis powers were defeated and the continent was liberated.

German-made U.S. Army Headquarters Europe patch in reverse

executing the destruction of Axis forces on the European Continent. After American forces were established in Europe, SHAEF assumed those responsibilities and this command became increasingly involved with the administration of service and supply. To reflect its new direction, the Service of Supply insignia was added to the top center of the patch between the lightning bolts. Eventually, the unit would assume another title and become Headquarters European Theater of Operations and adopted the 3rd style patch. ***Bottom row- left:*** English-made variation of the HQETO (3rd style) patch. Note the eagle faces right - $45.00. ***Right:*** Standard HQETO patch $20.00. Aside from SHAEF, this was the senior command in the European Theater.

European Theater of Operations

Top row – left: 2nd style, English-made patch. This variation is printed on cloth - $12.00. ***Middle:*** Standard 2nd style - $5.00. The 2nd style patch is also referred to as Communications Zone ETO. Tabs can be found that were made for wear underneath the 2nd style patch. These feature names like "OISE" (France), and are normally yellow embroidered details on blue material, with a blue border. Another tab made for wear above the patch reads "ADSEC" (Advanced Sector). This tab has yellow embroidered details on black material. ***Right:*** Standard 1st style patch - $15.00. *Service:* Originally, this command was tasked with planning and

Womens' Army Corps (WAC) Sergeant - Mary Knox.

Mary Knox served in the European Theater during WWII. She was involved in radio intelligence work and was a student of the Japanese language. Sgt. Knox has the distinction of having won two Purple Hearts for wounds received in action. An English made, 2nd style, ETO patch is clearly visible on her left shoulder, in this 1945 photograph..

General Headquarters South Pacific variations

Left Standard type with dark blue flag - $8.00. **Center** Standard type with medium blue flag - $8.00. **Right** Standard type with purple flag - $10.00. The letters became more stylized and the flag color was changed from blue to purple when the war ended. *Service:* This headquarters was a multinational command under the leadership of General Douglas MacArthur. It was responsible for the defense of Australia, recapturing the Philippines, military operations in the India area, and military operations in the pacific.

Allied Force Headquarters

Standard type - $5.00. A joint British and American command. *Service:* It controlled allied forces and supervised the invasions of North Africa, Sicily, Southern France, and controlled operations in the Mediterranean until the surrender of Germany.

North African Theater

Standard type - $6.00. *Service:* Primarily responsible for overseeing the preparation, training, and organization of forces for the North African campaigns. It later moved to Sicily and Italy, and finally assumed control of the Mediterranean Theater of Operations.

Middle East Forces

Standard design - $8.00. *Service:* Responsible for supporting the Ninth Army Air Force until its departure from the Middle East Theater. It then supported operations of the Air Transport Command to include activities in Northwest Africa.

Bullion China Burma India (CBI) patches and other CBI-made insignia

Six examples of bullion CBI patches. Note the different weaves and materials. On the bottom, left to right, are bullion Captain's bars, a Chinese Air Force officer's cap device, and a dragon insignia. Bullion CBI patches may range from $25.00 - $85.00 depending on the material and condition.

Reverse side of a theater made CBI patch.

An interesting characteristic of Asian made insignia is the frequent use of paper for backing material. In this particular case, the backing is newspaper. Some of the backing is in English, and the other is Indian. The English portion is not exposed to view but the Indian characters are visible in the illustration. This construction technique has continued and many years later, a large proportion of Vietnamese made insignia would be made using newspaper backing.

Fully embroidered variations of the CBI patch

Five fully embroidered variations - $6.00 each. Although subtle, there are differences in size, width, and the blue circle within the sun. The discrepancies in minor details are the "signatures" of different manufacturers. Note that the manufacturer who produced the middle patch, simply left the blue circle area bare allowing the dark blue field to show. The other manufacturers actually sew the circle onto the patch using light or medium-blue thread.

Oversize leather versions of the CBI patch were made for wear on flight jackets. These can measure as much as 9"x11", and were worn on the back. Other flight jacket insignia called "blood chits" were common in the CBI area. These usually incorporate some combination of Chinese, American, Indian, or Burmese flags with messages in the respective languages. The messages explained that the wearer was an ally and asked natives to render aid and facilitate the wearer's safe return to friendly lines. Blood chits may be leather, silk, or cloth. In many instances base commanders required the wearing of the blood chits and they could be obtained at the exchange, or from the native manufacturer. In some cases, as many as three different chits were required for wear both on the inside and outside of the jacket. Each one would be in a different language and bearing a different national emblem. This was necessary because flight crews may find themselves over China, Burma, or India on any given mission.

More examples of theater made CBI patches

These examples include printed, hand embroidered, machine woven, and leather. Top row types - $35.00 - $45.00. For leather types - $75.00.

There is probably no other American insignia from WWII that exists in as many variations as the CBI patch. Although several examples are illustrated, the different types are quite literally endless. Silk, metal, bullion, tinsels, twisted chord, leather, and other materials were all commonly used in the CBI area. With some expertise, it is possible to determine with some certainty which country the patch originated from based upon the materials and style. *Service:* CBI had responsibility for all U.S. troops on the Asiatic mainland. Additionally, it was responsible for training Chinese troops and maintaining an atmosphere of mutual cooperation with the Chinese leadership.

Note the hand embroidered enlisted discs on the lapels; "US" on the left and a winged propeller on the right. The corporal chevrons are hand embroidered in white on a background material identical to the jacket material. The CBI patch is a printed example with snaps on the reverse. This allowed the patch to be easily removed prior to laundering.

CBI made bush jacket

Executive Headquarters China

This patch is included because it appears in most WWII patch books. It is actually a post-war design introduced in January 1946. It was worn for approximately one year by a diplomatic mission attempting to work with both the Nationalist and Communist Chinese factions.

Close-up of enlisted discs on lapel

A classic example of the Indian made bush jacket. This example was worn by a corporal in the Army Air Force.

Ledo Road

Standard type - $20.00. *Service:* The Ledo Road became a military undertaking of immense proportions. The

(sometimes called the Stillwell Road) stretched from Ledo, India, to China, and took three years to complete. Prior to the road being opened, the only method of transporting supplies to China, was by aircraft. This patch was authorized for local wear and was not an approved design.

Pacific Ocean Areas

This patch has an unusual weave. It may have been produced in Australia.- $6.00. *Service:* This command had the responsibility for the administration and support of all U.S. forces in the central and south pacific areas. The Command also was involved in the planning and execution of combat operations.

Theater made variations of the Ledo Road patch

Both designs are crudely embroidered - $100.00 each. There is no meaning attached to the variation in colors. Each piece is the native artist's interpretation. Other examples exist in painted leather and are composed of several pieces sewn together. For a leather example - $100.00 - $150.00.

Western Pacific Forces variations

Left: Theater made with bullion and tinsel on felt. The patch is thick and very attractive - $60.00. **Right:** Standard type - $7.00. *Service:* This command had responsibility for the administration and support of American forces in the Western Pacific areas. It later became the Philippine - Ryukus Command.

(2nd design)   *(1st design)*
Southeast Asia Command

Standard type, 2nd design - $6.00. This Command was responsible for operations against Japanese forces in Southeast Asia, and creating over-land communications from India to China. It was primarily a joint British and American operation. The patch can be found with the phoenix facing both right and left. There is some evidence that the patch was originally produced with the right facing phoenix, and then changed to the phoenix facing left. There is also some evidence that this patch was worn on both shoulders by some personnel (all British personnel), which necessitated a right and left version to keep the phoenix facing to the wearer's front (Dexter). For a right facing phoenix (1st design) - $45.00.

Philippine Department

Standard type - $7.00. *Service:* This department was responsible for defending the Philippine Islands and for organizing and training an army. This patch was adopted in the 1920s and was utilized after the war ended. However, for the purposes of WWII historians, the Philippine Department was, for all intents and purposes, "lost in action" in 1942.

Guam Forces

Standard type - $35.00. *Service:* This patch was adopted after the Americans re-captured Guam from Japanese forces. Guam became an enormously busy and important port for forces in the pacific. This organization was responsible for managing the flow of supplies and other logistical matters on the Island. There is a smaller, circular patch of similar design that replaced this patch after the war.

Military Forces Japanese War Crimes Trials

Some sources claim that this patch was worn by military personnel involved with the war crime trials. It has been hotly contested by collectors for years. As far as I have been able to determine, no such patch was ever worn during the war crime trials. A rectangular tab was worn and came in one color for officers and another for enlisted personnel. After the war, patches like the one shown were produced in the Philippines as souvenirs for GIs returning home. This particular patch is made with copper metal thread and embroidery on felt. Despite the fact that these patches do not appear to be genuine WWII pieces, they bring outrageous prices. For a Philippine embroidered type - $300.00 - $500.00. The patch above is suspect because the same vendor had other WWII patch designs executed in an identical fashion. Some of these designs were European theater units, and others were in the pacific.

Military Mission to Moscow

Standard type - $30.00. *Service:* This command was originally organized to supervise Lend-Lease activities to the U.S.S.R.. Later, the command was given the unenviable task of attempting to secure some strategic coordination of military activities between the U.S.S.R. and the United Sates.

Military District of Washington

Standard type - $4.00. *Service:* This command was established to orchestrate the defense of Washington D.C.. As the war progressed, the organization assumed a role more like that of a Service Command.

Antilles Department

Standard type - $12.00. *Service:* This Command was responsible for the defense of Puerto Rico and the Virgin Islands.

Caribbean Defense Command

Standard type - $6.00. *Service:* The Command was responsible for activities in and around the Puerto Rico and Panama Canal Zones. Several departments, base commands, and the Sixth Army Air Force fell under the command of CDC.

Atlantic Base Command

Standard type - $8.00. *Service:* These commands were part of a defensive ring of outposts stretching from Newfoundland to the Caribbean. The "ABC's" personnel were primarily concentrated in the Caribbean zone.

Greenland Base Command

Standard type - $6.00. *Service:* The Command was organized with the cooperation of the Danish Government. It was largely responsible for the defense of the Greenland territory.

Bermuda Base Command

Standard type - $10.00. *Service:* This Command provided defense against enemy forces and submarine activities in the Bermuda area.

Iceland Base Command (Indigo Task Force) variations

Left: Standard type with Army Green border. This patch continued to be worn into the 1960s. This accounts for the Army Green border, which establishes this patch as being 1957 vintage or newer - $2.00. **Right:** A standard WWII type - $5.00. *Service:* This command was responsible for the defense of Iceland.

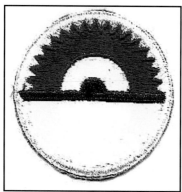

Labrador, NE Canada Base Command
Standard type - $7.00. *Service:* The command was responsible for the defense of Northeast Canada, Labrador and later, some of central Canada.

South Atlantic Forces
Left: Standard type - $10.00. **Right:** Overseas-made variation of unknown origin. This patch is produced with bullion thread on a brown, velvet-like backing - $60.00. *Service:* This command had the responsibility of creating a cooperative relationship with the Brazilian Government, and supporting the Air Transport Command in that area.

Quatermaster Corps
Standard type - $10.00. *Service:* This patch was worn by security personnel and workers at the numerous military

Victory Task Force
Standard type - $15.00. *Service:* This patch was worn by a group of soldiers who were essentially an army "road show". The troops conducted military maneuvers for the public and VIPs. Weapons were demonstrated and precision movements of personnel and vehicles were also featured. The purpose was to raise funds for the Army Emergency Relief Fund, but the extraordinary competence and capability of this unit was found to enhance citizen morale and confidence as well. The unit was disbanded prior to the war's end.

Veterans Administration
Standard type - $8.00. *Service:* The Veterans Administration (VA) was tasked with managing the many services and programs made available to military veterans. Medical care, benefits, loans, and other services were administered by the VA. This patch was authorized for wear by military personnel assigned to VA facilities.

Army Hostess and Librarian

Standard type - $20.00. *Service:* This program was developed during WWI, and continued in graduating degrees throughout WWII. The Army Hostesses were responsible for developing recreation and morale enhancing activities for GIs. The Hostesses served overseas as well as in the United States. I have never interviewed a man or woman that served during WWII, who did not take advantage of, and remember fondly, the services provided by the Hostesses.

ribbon. This complete uniform is the only example that I have encountered. This patch is very rare. The uniform is ultra rare - $750.00.

Women's Army Auxiliary Corps (later, the Women's Army Corps)

Women's Army Auxiliary Drivers Corps (WAADC)

This uniform was worn by a staff sergeant in the WAADC, a forerunner to the WAACs (eventually WACs). Examples of their duties included serving as messengers and providing transportation for high ranking officers and VIPs. I am aware of nine different location tabs for wear with this patch. All are central or southern California cities. Note the distinctive service stripes on the cuffs, the matched pair of WAADC distinctive insignia, and the embroidered

Women's Army Corps (WACs) in France, 1945

These three officers (nurses) are assigned to the European Theater of Operations Communication Zone. They are somewhere in France, playfully showing off the helmets that were just issued to them. Formerly the Women's Army Auxiliary Corps, WACs served in many capacities in every theater of war. Despite a prohibition on combat activities, more than 150 WACs were killed, wounded or missing in action.

French Forces Training in The United States

Standard type - $6.00. A smaller version of this patch is also fairly common. *Service:* Worn by French military personnel undergoing air combat training in the United States. All aspects of ground support and combat crew functions were offered to French personnel. Upon completion of the courses, the students were returned for service in the European Theater of Operations.

Army Specialized Training Reserve Program / Army Specialized Training Program

Left: Standard type ASTP (Reserve) in two-piece construction - $15.00. This patch also exists in a one-piece, fully embroidered construction, and embroidered on felt. **Right:** ASTP standard type - $8.00. *Service:* The ASTP (Reserve) performed a function similar to a high school ROTC program. It provided military training to young people and prepared them for military service. Students were inducted to the Armed Forces upon reaching their eighteenth birthday. The ASTP was tasked with preparing military personnel for advanced schools like Officer Candidate School, or other specialized training programs.

ASTP (Reserve) patch in reverse

This is an interesting example because it involves a regular ASTP patch being sewn to a background patch, which is simply a larger yellow square. It also allows collectors to see how fully embroidered, WWII period patches were constructed. In this case, a piece of khaki colored base material was covered with yellow thread around the edges. The middle was not covered because the ASTP patch, once sewn onto the square, would cover the center area that was left bare. WWII patches are merely sheets of base fabric, like the tan khaki material visible here, that had patch designs sewn onto them in colored threads. Rows and rows of a particular patch design would be sewn and then later cut into separate squares, with one patch per square. The excess base material would then be trimmed around the edges of each patch. The only remaining trace of the base fabric is visible by looking at the extreme edge of the patch where, normally, khaki or olive drab material can be seen.

Officer Candidate School variations

Top Row - Left: Standard type error design with backward "S". Light brown letters on black - $15.00. **Middle:**

Standard type with light green letters on black - $5.00. *Right:* Standard type with medium brown letters on dark blue - $5.00. **Bottom Row - Left:** Standard type with dark green letters on medium blue - $10.00. **Right:** Standard women's type with gold-yellow letters on black - $8.00. *Service:* OCS provided leadership training to warrant officers and enlisted men who had exhibited outstanding leadership traits and who were considered to be good candidates for commissions as officers. This patch was displayed on the shirt pocket, or on the sleeve when a jacket was worn.

Both are standard types although the patch on the left is WWII vintage, and the patch on the right is pre-war. Both are embroidered on wool - $8.00. This insignia was adopted prior to WWII, and by regulations, was to be dark blue letters on a shield that was the color of the uniform worn. Consequently, there are many variations in the color of this patch. Obviously, in the case of the patch on the left, if the school uniform was a dark blue or black and the shield needed to be the same color, dark blue letters would not work. *Service:* ROTC was a college based program, which allowed students to prepare themselves for service as reserve military officers.

Military Academy (West Point)

Standard type - $6.00. *Service:* The Academy was responsible for training cadets to be military officers and to prepare them for military careers. This included Army Air Force officers as well. During WWII, because of the urgent demand for qualified, capable officers, the course was reduced in duration from four years to three.

Airborne Command

Standard type - $8.00. This patch can be found with the aircraft facing right - $50.00. *Service:* The Airborne Command was based at Fort Benning, Georgia and was responsible for training all airborne forces, which included parachute infantry, glider infantry and artillery troops.

Reserve Officer's Training Corps (ROTC) variations

UNITED STATES ARMY AIR FORCES

WWII saw an emphasis on air power that would have seemed preposterous only a few years before. The American Air Force expanded to such an incredible extent that it eventually warranted a five-star general as commander (Hap Arnold). There are a number of officially recognized patches worn by the Army Air Forces. There are others which were worn on a large scale and, although not officially adopted, they are familiar enough to be recognized in most publications dealing with WWII insignia. This book concentrates on those insignia. Almost every air division, wing, group, and squadron had an unofficial patch of their own. These were worn on flight clothing and utilities. The sheer number of unofficial unit patches makes including them in this book impossible. However, the collector should be aware that these. Group and squadron patches are getting very hard to find and are extremely desirable. Prices in the $200.00 - $350.00 dollar range are the norm. Examples can be found in every style and material imaginable. Leather, painted, cloth, chenille, bullion, canvas, embroidered, silk and more. These patches frequently tend to be larger on average, because they were usually worn on the chest of jackets or overalls. In this book I have included patches from most of the major commands, all of the numbered air forces, and the specialist designators.

England was a source for many beautiful variations of American insignia. This is particularly true for resident Army Air Force units. The Eighth and Ninth Army Air Forces are good examples. Countless variations of these patches exist including printed, leather, bullion on felt, and embroidered designs.

The U.S. Air Force discontinued the use of shoulder patches on service and dress uniforms in 1947, when it became a separate arm of service. But, the tradition has continued through the use of cloth insignia worn as pocket patches or shoulder patches on flight clothing and utilities.

As was mentioned, the prices of WWII flying unit insignia are very high. Values in the hundreds of dollars are common. The collector needs to be particularly cautious when purchasing these items. Collectors not only have to concern themselves with the abundance of reproductions on the market, but they must also identify more recent designs represented as being WWII vintage. There is a huge disparity in value between flying insignia of WWII, and even the Korean War just a few years later. The age and appearance of patches from both these periods can be almost identical. Reputable dealers, experience, and provenance are the best insurance in these cases. Pay close attention to the type of manufacture and materials. Compare WWII service locations of flying units with the common material and construction styles originating from those areas during the war. Remember that a lot of group, squadron and other flying related insignia were manufactured in the U.S. as well as overseas. Beware of AAF designs that are executed in a copper/bronze colored bullion. Gold and silver bullion were the predominant materials used during WWII. There are a number of high quality reproductions on the market in the copper style construction. Close examination may be required because aged gold bullion can assume an appearance very similar to copper or bronze. One of the most important investigative techniques involves knowing that a particular unit existed during WWII and where it served. There are a number of books on the market that list all of the AAF units from 1941-1945, and provide service summaries for each. **Note:** A WW II vintage Sixteenth Army Air Force patch can be found. It is unknown if this patch was manufactured in error, or if there was some official anticipation of organizing this unit. These are often listed as purely reproduction, but some vintage designs exist and they are absolutely authentic much like the army phantom types. Originals are executed in a light blue and the design resembles that of the 15th Army Air Force. These are quite rare - $200.00+.

General Headquarters Air Force

Felt on felt type - $30.00. *Service:* Responsible for overseeing the development and selection of bombardment aircraft. It later assumed control of all combat aircraft in the nation's inventory. Eventually, it became the headquarters for the United States Army Air Forces. This insignia was worn from 1937 - 1942.

purple wool. Both gold and silver bullion were used in this example. This patch originated from the China Burma India (CBI) Theater of Operations - $45.00. Many factory embroidered variations can be found including types with radical color combinations such as an orange disc rather than the blue. Others have no red dot in the middle of the star. The variations have differing values and there are too many to list. But $45.00 is probably an appropriate average value.

Army Air Force novelty patch

Novelty patches came in a variety of sizes and styles with the generic branch of service types being the most common. These patches were private-purchase items available at the post exchange or tailor/uniform supply shops. This example measures 4" across and is worn on a jacket. This piece is embroidered on a thin, silky material with a cheese cloth backing $10.00.

Army Air Forces *Army Air Forces in bullion*
Left: American embroidered on felt (note moth nips on lower edge) - $4.00. **Right:** Bullion thread on a coarse

Aviation Cadet (blue)

Aviation Cadets (black)

Top: Standard type - $5.00. **Left:** Embroidered on felt - $8.00. **Right:** standard, fully embroidered type - $5.00. This patch was worn by flying cadets as well as personnel who were engaged in certain specialized technical training programs. It was worn on the left shoulder of the shirt. On the service blouse, the patch was worn on the lower right sleeve. There is confusion as to why this insignia can be found in both blue and black. Some suggest that one color was worn by cadets specializing in ground functions and the other was worn by flying cadets. I have seen photographic evidence that seems to contradict this theory. Another variation features the wing design stenciled on khaki canvas.

forces in the United Kingdom. It eventually controlled the Eighth, Ninth, and to some extent, the Fifteenth Army Air Force. This command supervised the strategic bombing campaigns across Europe, and the strategic sorties flown in support of the Normandy invasion.

Ninth Engineer Command (advance)

Standard type - $12.00. *Service:* Was originally organized as part of the Ninth Army Air Force. The command steadily grew in size and eventually controlled multiple engineer regiments and battalions. This command was responsible for the construction of new airfields, and the rehabilitation of captured and existing airfields as the allied forces swept across Europe. This command included airborne engineer battalions. The airborne battalion members were additionally authorized to wear a red and white Airborne tab above the Ninth Engineer Command insignia. For an airborne example with tab - $35.00.

United States Strategic Air Forces Europe

Standard type - $20.00. *Service:* (Formerly 8th Army Air Force) was responsible for the administration of all air

Far East Air Forces

Left: Australian-made, embroidered on a dark blue, vertically ribbed embroidered base - $12.00. **Middle:** This

is the light blue American-made variation - $30.00. **Right:** Standard type - $4.00. *Service:* Was organized in Australia and charged with the responsibility of coordinating and controlling the Fifth and Thirteenth Army Air Forces. The Seventh Army Air Force joined the command later. The command served in Japan with occupation forces as well.

Air Corps Ferrying Command

This is the miniature variation for wear on the cap - $6.00. *Service:* Responsible for transporting aircraft from production sites to staging areas, hauling cargo, transporting aircraft to combat units, and other service activities. The red and blue lines at the top of the patch represent morse code (dots and dashes). The morse code represents "ACFC". This command was redesignated later to the Air Forces Ferrying Command. The morse code was changed on the patch to represent the new title "AFFC". The example shown has ACFC morse code.

Mediterranean Allied Air Forces

Standard type - $10.00. *Service:* Was organized when all allied air assets in the Mediterranean zone were merged. Aside from British RAF units, the command controlled the Twelfth and Fifteenth Army Air Forces.

Two examples of Italian-made Mediterranean Army Air Force patches

These are fairly typical of Italian-made bullion variations - $75.00 each.

Air Force Air Transport Command

Standard type - $6.00. *Service:* Assumed the duties of the Ferrying Command and was also charged with transporting troops and supplies all over the world. The ATC incorporated military and civilian contract personnel. Note that the blue and red lines at the top of the patch, representing morse code, have been changed to AFATC.

Desert Air Force

An extremely nice example with embroidered details on a RAF-blue felt base - $50.00. *Service:* Served in North Africa, Sicily, and Italy. Although a primarily British organization, some American units served with the DAF.

group flew P-47 "Thunderbolts". Period unit histories are a great source of information on the insignia (official and unofficial) utilized by various organizations.

87th Fighter Squadron insignia illustrated in the 79th Fighter Group History.

Cover page from the The Falcon, Combat History of the 79th Fighter Group *(otherwise unattributed, 1946).*

This is the cover page from a unit history detailing the wartime exploits of the 79th Fighter Group. The illustrated patches signify service during the war with the 9th AAF, 12th AAF, and the Desert Air Force. The bird design is the insignia adopted by the 79th Fighter Group. It is Horus the Hawk, which is taken from Ancient Egyptian history. Egypt is where this unit experienced combat for the first time. The

More examples of insignia illustrations found in period books

These are from the book – ***The Story of the 390th Bomb Group (H)**, 1947, (otherwise unattributed).* **Top left:** 568th Squadron ***Top right:*** 569th Squadron **Middle:** 390th Bombardment Group (H) (meaning Heavy bombers) ***Bottom left:*** 570th Squadron. ***Bottom right:*** 571st Squadron. Like this one, unit histories often have full color, detailed illustrations, which are of obvious value to a collector. Additionally, the photographs of personnel and activities often show the insignia being worn. Variations are also commonly found in the pictures including painted renditions on flight jackets, and other improvised designs.

———⚬⚬⚬———

Second Army Air Force

Standard type - $4.00. *Service:* (Formerly Northwest Air District) was responsible for the defense of the West Coast and training activities.

Front and reverse sides of English-made Airborne Troop Carrier patch

Typical English-made example. Embroidered on felt - $45.00. Note the indentations around the edge caused by thread that once bound the patch to a uniform. *Service:* Responsible for the delivery of airborne units in operations ranging in size from the Market Garden and D-Day drops, to one-man drops conducted by the Office of Strategic Services (OSS). This command included motorized transport like the C-47, and glider aircraft like the Horsa.

———⚬⚬⚬———

Third Army Air Force

Left: Unusual light-yellow variation with ribbed weave - $20.00. **Right:** Standard type - $4.00. *Service:* (Formerly Southeast Air District) was responsible for the defense of the Southeastern states, Gulf area and training activities.

First Army Air Force variations

Left: American embroidered on felt. Note a couple moth nips around edge - $4.00. **Right:** Standard type - $4.00. *Service:* (Formerly Northeast Air District) was responsible for defending the Eastern Seaboard and training activities.

Fourth Army Air Force

Standard type - $4.00. *Service:* (Formerly Southwest Air District) was responsible for the defense of the Southwestern United States and training activities.

Unknown technician wearing 4th Army Air Force patch and Engineer disc on left lapel, 1944.

chute qualified personnel. They were organized to provide medical assistance and conduct rescue operations involving downed airmen. For an example with articulated provenance - $250.00. **Right:** Standard type - $5.00. *Service:* (Formerly Philippine Department Air Force) Philippines, Australia, New Guinea, various island campaigns, Okinawa, occupation duty in Japan. The 5th Army Air Force saw extensive service in Korea during the Korean War. Consequently, thousands of bullion variations of the 5th Army Air Force patch were produced in Korea. Some have an attached arc over the top with "KOREA" also done in bullion. When purchasing a bullion 5th Air Force patch it may be all but impossible to determine with certainty if it is WWII or Korean vintage. The fact is, there is no difference in price or value associated with either period, and the examples from both are masterfully executed and equally attractive.

Sixth Army Air Force

Standard type - $5.00. *Service:* (Formerly Panama Canal Air Force) was responsible for the defense of the Caribbean area to include the Panama Canal. It performed training activities and maintained stations in Central and South America.

Fifth Army Air Force

Left: Very rare 5th Army Air Force Airborne rescue. This airborne tab is cut differently to accommodate the curve of the 5th AAF patch. In many cases the ends of the tab will be cut at an angle approaching forty-five degrees. The letters on the tab tend to be more gray than white. The difference in color is noticeable and can be distinguished simply by looking. *Service:* This was a small detachment of para-

Seventh Army Air Force

Standard type - $5.00. *Service:* (Formerly Hawaiian Air Force) was responsible for the defense of Hawaii. It assisted

in combat at Midway and Wake. It later served in the Guadalcanal, Gilbert and Marshall Islands, Saipan, Guam, Philippines, Okinawa, and other island campaigns.

in England. The 8th Army Air Force patch has been hand-embroidered on silk. The words "Greetings from England" appear around the patch. Although attractive, these items generally remain surprisingly inexpensive - $20.00.

8th Army Air Force

Standard type - $8.00. *Service:* Primarily a strategic (bomber) command. It was based in England and conducted the air campaign against Axis targets on the European Continent to include Norway, Holland, Belgium, France, and Germany. Toward the end of the war in Europe, the Eighth could muster over 3,000 aircraft for a single mission. When Germany surrendered, the command moved to Okinawa. The Japanese capitulated shortly thereafter. Thousands of Eighth Army Air Force variations exist, which were produced in England. Many are of bullion on felt, silk thread on felt, or leather construction. Elaborate bullion designs are now averaging $55.00 - $150.00 (more for truly exceptional designs).

Ninth Army Air Force variations
Left: American embroidered type in unusually rigid weave - $6.00. **Middle:** English-made, hand embroidered in silky thread, on a felt base - $45.00. **Right:** Standard type - $6.00. *Service:* North Africa, Sicily, Italy, Rumania and England.

10th Army Air Force variations
Top: Bullion example produced in India. It is done in heavy silver and gold bullion, on black wool - $85.00. On the black wool you will note a white circle around the patch. This is a maker-applied stencil to serve as a guide when trimming the excess away in preparation for wear. Bullion variations of the 10th, 14th, and 20th Air Forces are common as they all did extended service in the China, Burma, India areas. **Bottom left:** Standard type - $6.00. **Bottom right:** Another example from India, but this patch is made from nine pieces of leather. The colors are applied in paint. This example is also unused. These

English, hand embroidered 8th AAF doily
An example of patch designs that can be found on souvenir items sent home by GIs. This is a doily manufactured

10th Air Force patches belonged to Sgt. Henry W. Berquist. Mr. Berquist served as a gunner on B-17s based in India. *Service:* China, Burma, India.

Indian made 10th Air Force patch

This is a fairly common variation of the 10th Air Force patch originating from India. It is hand-embroidered on a blue twill - $40.00.

Eleventh Army Air Force

Standard type - $6.00. *Service:* (Formerly Alaskan Air Force) Was responsible for the defense of Alaska. The Eleventh fought in the Aleutian Islands, and Northern Japanese held islands.

Twelfth Army Air Force / Twelfth Tactical Command

Left: Standard type - $5.00. The Twelfth Air Force served in North Africa, Sicily, Italy, France. ***Right::*** Embroidered on felt with cheesecloth backing. Probably English made - $30.00. *Service:* The Twelfth Tactical Command served in Italy, North Africa, France, Belgium, and Germany. Some experts insist that this design was never worn. Others have insisted it was worn under local authority. The latter group is correct. I have a period photograph showing an officer wearing this design in the presence of another AAF Captain, and a Major or Lieutenant Colonel. There is also a British officer present. The photograph was taken in an urban setting in France.

Thirteenth Army Air Force

Standard type - $6.00. *Service:* New Caledonia, Australia, island campaigns including Guadalcanal, Solomons, New Georgia, New Britain, Carolines, New Guinea, and others around the Philippines. Components of this command relocated to Okinawa as well.

Fourteenth Army Air Force

Standard type - $7.00. *Service:* China, Burma, India area and replaced the famous American Volunteer Group (Flying Tigers). The AVG was a small group of volunteer American pilots that served in China prior to formal U.S. intervention there. Many of their aircraft cowlings were decorated with large shark-mouths, complete with jagged teeth and eyes. The flying tiger nickname resulted from this paint scheme. The AVG adopted a design like this one in many of their insignia. Scarves, painted jackets, and patches were adorned with a "Flying Tiger". Insignia attributable to the AVG are quite rare. Flying tiger patches that have an indisputable provenance from the AVG may sell for $800.00+. When the 14th Air Force absorbed the AVG, the design was continued in the shoulder patch. These standard issue patches are often times advertised as "Flying Tiger patches", but they have no association to the AVG and are very common. Because the 14th served in the China, Burma, India theater, thousands of gorgeous bullion examples exist as well as leather, silk and hand-embroidered types. A bullion 14th Air Force patch may sell for $75.00 - $!25.00.

Fifteenth Army Air Force

Standard type - $7.00. ***Service:*** Originally formed in North Africa and attacked targets in Italy, Germany, Austria, Czechoslovakia, Poland and other locations during the war. Leather examples of the 15th Army Air Force tend to be more scarce than the other Air Forces serving in Europe and the Mediterranean areas.

Another 15th Air Force design (unofficial) exists and was worn for approximately one month in 1943. This patch is shield shaped, has a blue horizontal rectangle at top, with the winged star across the rectangle. The lower two-thirds of the shield is normally yellow with red Roman numerals XV stretching from the bottom of the blue rectangle to the bottom of the patch. Many of these were done with bullion wings and numerals. Other examples can be found in leather - $250.00.

Eighteenth Army Air Force

This patch was produced soley for collectors as a novelty patch. This example is embroidered on twill - $1.00.

Service: This organization did not exist. It is illustrated here because these patches are found for sale to collectors and they are represented at times as being of WWII vintage or "ghost air force" types. They have no value.

Twentieth Army Air Force

consisted primarily of B-29 bombers and their escorts. This command maintained bases on Tinian, Guam, and Saipan, from which it flew strategic missions against Japan. It also attacked targets in the Burma area.

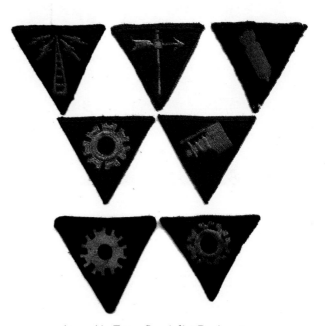

Army Air Force Specialist Designators

These designs were worn by personnel who had received specialized training and/or possessed an inordinate level of skill. These patches were worn on the lower right sleeve of the service tunic, or on the left pocket of the fatigue shirt. ***From top - left to right:*** Communications Specialist (radio tower) / Weather Specialist (weather vane) / Armament Specialist (bomb) / Engineering Specialist (engine) / Photography Specialist (camera) / Engineering Specialist made in China, Burma, India Theater, printed yellow engine on blue muslin / Engineering Specialist embroidered on twill with cheesecloth backing. For the first five (standard types) - $4.00. For the CBI made printed type - $12.00. For the embroidered on twill type - $5.00.

Italian-made Communications Specialist designator.
Bullion on blue felt - $20.00

reproduction squadron insignia

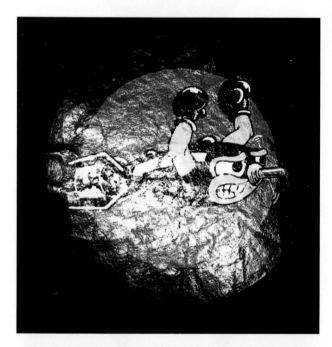

These are examples of reproduction WWII leather squadron insignia. ***First:*** A bomber squadron type, which is hand painted on leather. The patch has needle holes around the edge suggesting that it had been removed from a jacket. Close examination disclosed that there were no signs of distortion in the needle holes where thread would have created tension, and elongated one area of each hole. Furthermore, there were no indentations where the thread would have extended between holes, or from the holes to the edge of the patch. Finally, the thread would have scuffed the paint over time, where it bound into the leather design. The holes were created with a "dry" needle and were done to create an illusion of use. This patch was $200.00 and offered as an original through a reputable dealer.

Second: A fighter squadron design. The white thread used to assemble separate leather components was covered with a magic marker on the front of the patch. This seemed to be intended to blend the white thread with the rest of the design. However the white thread on the reverse had not been colored. When exposed to ultraviolet light it reacted and was obviously synthetic. This reproduction was priced at $200.00 and was offered as an original by a reputable dealer.

Third: Another bomber squadron type. It is also hand painted on leather. The face of this patch was lightly scuffed and had an appearance of use. When examined closely however, the wear was found to be as prevalent to the valleys of the leather, as it was to the peaks. This should raise suspicion because normal use would cause scuffs to the paint across the high points of the leather where things would routinely rub against the design. It is reasonable to conclude that only deliberate scuffing by use of a brush or other device would affect the paint in the recesses. The authenticity of this design is highly suspect. This patch was priced at $200.00 and was offered as authentic by a reputable dealer.

I am quite certain that the dealer assumed them to be "right". But dealers cannot be expected to scrutinize every piece in minute detail. It pays to become an expert in your interest. These three patches alone represent $600.00 in worthless purchases. The advantage of dealing with reputable dealers is their willingness to refund or exchange items if the buyer is dissatisfied. Had these been purchased at a flea market or gun show, the only outcome would have been a devastating loss of money. Remember that the people most likely to spend this much money for a patch are serious collectors and dealers. Should you decide to sell a patch, or even your collection, expensive items will be thoroughly scrutinized by these experts. If you hope to see an appreciation of your investment, and if you seek confidence in your ability to recover the investment, you need to possess the same expertise that future buyers are likely to possess.

ers to continue beyond these targets to Russian airfields where they could be re-fueled and re-armed, not only allowing them to strike these targets, but also making it possible to execute a mission on the return trip. A small contingent of Americans were assigned to these airfields to coordinate activities and provide ground support. The program was a disaster and Russian cooperation was reluctant at best. Some personnel assigned to this program had these patches made. They are an unauthorized design intended for local wear only. Very few original examples are known to exist. This patch falls into the ultra rare category.

Eagle Squadron, Front and Reverse

This is an English-made Eagle Squadron patch, in silver bullion thread on black wool. The Eagle Squadron consisted of American volunteer aviators that flew combat missions for the RAF in England, prior to formal American involvement. Background colors include black and various shades of blue. This patch was worn on the sleeve - $250.00.

Air technical Service command

Standard type patch and tab - $8.00. *Service:* This command conducted training for support personnel and managed the inventory of the Army Air Forces.

Russian 8th Air Force Shuttle - Front and Reverse

Machine embroidered on felt - $750.00. The 8th Army Air Force identified a number of critical targets in Germany that were too distant to allow allied bombers to make the return trip to England. After negotiations with the Russians, it was arranged for the bomb-

Army Airways Communication System patch variations

Left: Standard fully embroidered patch and tab - $6.00. **Right:** Italian-made patch and tab. The patch is gold and silver bullion on a coarse wool. The tab is gold bullion on felt. For the set - $150.00. *Service:* The AACS became a major command in 1944. They were responsible for air traffic control towers and systems, communications facilities, weather facilities and other airways related support.

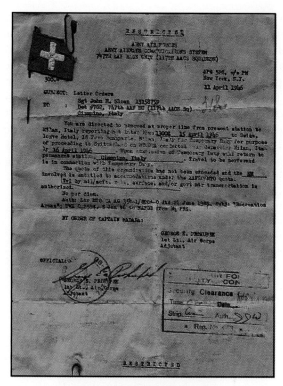

Women's Air Force Service Pilots

Standard type, embroidered on twill - $50.00. *Service:* WASPs were women that completed flight school minus some of the combat specific components. These women performed myriad duties including ferrying, training, courier duties, and other non-combatant functions. The Women's Auxiliary Ferrying Squadron (WAFS) was also composed of female aviators. Although the WAFS began as a separate organization, they were eventually absorbed by the WASPs.

AACS document

This document, dated 1946, directs Sgt. John H. Sloan to proceed from Italy to Switzerland. Documents like this one, which accompany a patch(s), help to determine the origin of the patch or corroborate the claim of the seller/owner. This document accompanied the Italian-made bullion AACS patch shown previously. The Swiss flag patch, which is pinned to the document, was intended for wear during travel. It allowed transportation personnel, whether it be train, plane or other, to ensure their passengers were on the proper vehicle and were proceeding to the correct destination. It also helped to overcome the language barriers when travelling through several countries. Transportation employees could glance at the flag, and direct GIs to the proper departure point and vehicle.

Contract Carrier Ground Personnel

Standard type - $20.00. *Service:* This patch can be found in many materials and sizes. This organization was composed of ground personnel working for the Air Transport Command.

Philippine Air Force

Standard type - $80.00. Worn by Philippine nationals training with American Air Force personnel.

Women's Auxiliary Ferrying Squadron (WAFS)

Standard type - $100.00. *Service:* The WAFS were trained female pilots who worked under the direction of the Air Transport Command. Their primary mission involved ferrying aircraft to domestic staging areas in preparation for overseas deployment.

Civil Air Patrol

Standard type - $10.00. *Service:* CAP was originally administered by the Office of Civilian Defense. CAP consisted of civilian pilots, ground personnel, and privately owned aircraft. These volunteers performed service to the war effort by conducting coastal anti-submarine patrols, search and rescue missions, and other operations that supplemented domestic military resources.

Reproduction copper bullion Army Air Force patches

These patches began surfacing some years ago and can be found in many WWII patch designs. You will note that the metal thread is clearly copper rather than the rich, heavy silver or gold bullion, which is characteristic of WWII vintage patches. I have had a number of experts explain that copper was indeed a popular material for patches during WWII. This is quite simply, absolutely, untrue. Although rare examples of copper may exist, they are extraordinarily unusual. These patches are reproductions and have no worth or historical value.

More examples of reproduction bullion patches

The felt background material is inferior to vintage material. The metal threads are conspicuously absent of age and patina. The reverse sides also appear new and crisp, unless artificially aged by an unscrupulous seller. Patches like these, executed in copper-like threads, are fakes. Pakistan, Singapore, and other countries still produce bullion insignia in enormous volumes. Many of these are in silver and/or gold, and more closely resemble WWII types. But after looking at original bullion patches, you will not be fooled by the inferior products manufactured today. The "bullion threads" of these modern types are often times not metal threads at all. And in fact, often look like plastic when examined closely. Most of the materials used currently are not vulnerable to patina and they will not exhibit the darkened, aged appearance that originals do. Many of these reproductions have white synthetic cheesecloth or threads on the reverse which will react to ultraviolet light and further establish the fact that they are of recent manufacture.

Order of the Goldfish (also referred to as Order of the Guppy)

Order of The Winged Boot/ Goldfish Club. These were unofficial patches associated with the AAF and Royal Air Force based in England. The first, is a likeness of a boot with outstretched wings. The second, shows a likeness of a fish with outstretched wings. Both may be embroidered or bullion on slate gray, olive drab, RAF blue, or black material. They vary in size but average about 2" square. They were unofficially worn to recognize aircrew members who were shot down and successfully evaded capture on the ground (winged boot) or successfully ditched in the English Channel (winged goldfish). These are both scarce pieces. $75.00 - $250.00

UNITED STATES MARINE CORPS, NAVY & COAST GUARD

United States Marine Corps "novelty" jacket patch

The Marine Corps adopted the bull dog as a mascot long ago. Consequently, the bull dog is frequently found on Marine Corps novelty items including insignia, jewelry, and clothing. This particular patch was sold at post exchanges and tailor shops catering to marines. Typically, this patch would be worn on the back or breast of a jacket. In this case, a white-felt bull dog silhouette is applied to a slightly larger red-felt bull dog silhouette. The black detail is printed in ink. The patch measures approximately 5-1/2" x 4-1/2". This WWII example is unused - $45.00.

More examples of USMC jacket patches

Left: Embroidered on white felt with mesh backing - $25.00 *Right:* Embroidered on maroon felt with mesh backing - $25.00.

Jacket patches in reverse showing white muslin backs

During WW I, the Marine Corps units assigned to the 2nd Division adopted colorful shoulder patch designs. The 5th Marine Brigade had patches of their own. Like other WWI insignia, different shapes and colors were incorporated to distinguish marine units, and frequently, to further identify the wearer's specific regiment, battalion, and so on. After that war the Marine Corps discontinued the use of shoulder sleeve insignia. In 1943, certain units were once again (officially) authorized to wear shoulder patches. This resulted in many of them adopting a design whether officially sanctioned or not. In 1947, the Marine Corps banned the use of shoulder patches once again. The rationale was quite simply that the Marine Corps has historically attempted to foster the belief that the entire "Corps" was one, unified team. It was felt that distinguishing between various units and specialties through the wearing of distinctive insignia, would to erode the unified spirit of the organization.

114

The types illustrated in this section were created and worn during WWII. Although many Marine Corps patches have been worn on an unofficial "local authority" basis since then, those shown here represent the widely used and recognized designs of the period. Naval personnel assigned to marine units were authorized to wear the shoulder insignia of that unit. This is most commonly associated with the many U.S. Navy medical personnel who have traditionally functioned as combat medics for the Marines. However, other Navy insignia were also worn in marine colors by construction battalion (Sea Bees) assigned to Fleet Marine Force units. Despite the marine uniform and organization patch, the Navy personnel utilized the standard Navy rate (enlisted rank) insignia that was modified in color to be consistent with the appearance of the Marine uniform. Other Navy specialty insignia were also manufactured and worn in marine red and green.

Because of the high prices paid for originals, Marine patches are frequently reproduced and misrepresented. Many of the Marine reproduction patches have an opaque glaze, called "sizing", applied to the reverse side or around the reverse edges. Sizing became a popular method of stiffening patches after the war. Patches with sizing applied to the back are most probably not of WWII manufacture. A few Marine patch designs have been used in later times on an unofficial basis. Therefore, there are newer versions of some Marine patches that are widely thought to have been unique to WWII.

USMC Fifth Corps (Amphibious) variations
Top Row - Left: Australian-made example embroidered on felt with mesh backing - $45.00. **Right:** Australian-made example, embroidered on twill with mesh backing - $45.00. **Bottom -** Standard type - $25.00. *Service:* Provided administrative control of logistics for marine units in the Central Pacific, and coordinated Marine and Army amphibious activities. It later served on occupation duty in Japan.

Fifth Amphibious Corps variation
A very unusual and, as yet, unexplained variation with a single star instead of the usual three stars - $50.00. One theory has it that this patch was worn by HQ personnel. Yet another suggested that this was a prototype and that the five-pointed star symbolized Fifth Corps, but that the accepted design bore three stars in honor of the 3-star General commanding. Yet another is that this was simply an error. Solving mysteries such as this are one of the joys of collecting. The *Trading Post* is a quarterly publication sent to members of the American Society of Military Insignia Collectors (ASMIC). One immensely valuable benefit to subscribing is the ability to send an image to the *Trading Post* staff

USMC Third Corps (Amphibious)
Standard type - $ 20.00. *Service:* was responsible for controlling all Marine forces in the Pacific. It replaced the First Corps in 1944. When Japan surrendered, this organization relocated to China.

for publication in a future issue. The image appears in the "Can You Identify" section. This gives every subscriber an opportunity to view it and respond with any information they may have. It also provides the other readers with the knowledge gained through these exchanges of information. Many ASMIC members possess an incredible wealth of information, some on specific units and others very generally. These people, collectively, represent the most priceless resource a collector has available.

51st Defense Battalion

Standard type - $20.00. *Service:* This battalion was initially at New River, North Carolina before moving to the Ellice Islands in the Pacific. It later moved to Eniwetok, and Kwajalein.

13th Defense Battalion

Standard type - $20.00. *Service:* This battalion was at Guantanamo Bay, Cuba prior to being sent to Hawaii. Eventually, it's personnel were reassigned to other units throughout the Pacific.

52nd Defense Battalion

Standard type - $20.00. *Service:* This battalion was also at New River, North Carolina, prior to being sent to the Marshall Islands.

18th Defense Battalion

Standard type - $20.00. *Service:* The battalion was initially assigned to New River, North Carolina. After some reorganization, It served on Tinian and Saipan.

Marine Detachments Afloat

Standard type - $25.00. *Service:* Marines have traditionally been assigned to larger naval vessels. They provide

116

security, act as gun crews, and serve when necessary as a landing force. This patch was authorized for wear by Marines posted aboard ship.

Marine Barracks Londonderry
Standard type - $25.00. If examined closely, the reader will see the indentations around the patch edge where thread bound it to a uniform at one time. This can be one characteristic of an original patch. *Service:* This unit was assigned to Naval Base Londonderry, Ireland.

First Marine Brigade (Iceland)
Standard English type, embroidered on felt - $25.00. *Service:* The brigade was responsible for the defense of Iceland. This was a joint operation with U.S. and British forces. This patch was a British design worn by their garrison on Iceland. It was adopted by the Marine detachment for local wear only. The British tradition is to wear their patch on both sleeves. Consequently, these patches were issued to Marines in pairs, and were worn on both sleeves as well. A pair consists of the bear facing opposing directions so that when worn on both sleeves the bear is always facing front (Dexter). A matched, uncut pair may sell for $60.00. The author has encountered several variations including printed types. This patch was later manufactured in the U.S. during the war. The patches had to be removed once the wearer left Iceland.

First Marine Division
Standard type - $12.00. *Service:* This was the first *division* ever designated as such by the Marine Corps. New Zealand, Guadalcanal (Solomon Islands), Australia, New Britain, Philippines, Okinawa, China, and other island campaigns. *Note*: There is a tab that was produced in extremely limited numbers for wear underneath the 1st Division patch. The Cape was a critical stepping-stone in the campaign to secure areas suitable for airfields, which would support future operations. The tab would have been used to distinguish division members that participated in the fighting on the Cape. The tab was proposed in early 1944, but after some debate and consideration, the request to wear the tab was withdrawn. Despite this, a few examples were produced, but they are very rare. Since 1998, reproduction tabs have surfaced everywhere. The collector needs to be very wary of any examples offered for sale. The collector should be prepared to pay $150.00+ for a period piece.

Second Marine Division (1st style)

Standard type - $20.00. This patch was worn unofficially. Despite an official design being approved for wear (below), this patch could be found in use throughout the war. *Service:* Florida Islands, Guadalcanal (Solomon Islands), Gilbert Islands, Marianas, Tinian, Saipan, Okinawa, Occupation duties

broidered on felt with a white hand - $40.00. *Right :* Australian embroidered type with very coarse weave and well defined fingers- $45.00.

Second Marine Division (error type)

This is a fully embroidered patch. It is often referred to as the "kidney" or "inverted heart" design. The patch was manufactured based upon an illustration in a period publication. The illustration was the result of a telephone conversation and is an interesting example of the disparity sometimes, between what one person thinks they said, and what another thinks they heard! Manufacturers who saw the illustration began producing the patch. Despite its radical departure from the official design it was actually purchased and worn by some members of the division. This patch has become fairly scarce - $200.00.

Second Marine Division variations (2nd style)

Top row – Left:: Standard type - $20.00. Note the fat flame, small "2", small stars, and gold hand. ***Right::*** Standard type - $20.00. There is a small moth nip in this patch between the left-hand star and the thumb. *Center:* Australian- made, embroidered on felt with a gold hand - $40.00. This patch is a bit oversized and has a vertical ribbed weave. ***Bottom row - Left:*** Australian-made, em-

Third Marine Division variations

Left: Embroidered on felt - $15.00. **Right:** Standard type: $8.00. *Service:* New Zealand, Guadalcanal, Solomon Islands, New Ireland, Guam, Marianas Islands, Iwo Jima, and island occupation duties. Many of the Marine Corps patches can be found in Australian, Japanese, and Chinese silk or bevo-like varieties. The Third Division however, is one of the most frequently found in those materials. For a bevo type: $45.00 - $80.00

Fourth Marine Division

Standard type - $10.00. One variation exists with a horizontal "foot" on the bottom of the "4"- $100.00. *Service:* Marshall Islands, Saipan, Tinian, Iwo Jima.

Fifth Marine Division variations
Left: Embroidered on felt - $25.00. **Center:** Standard type - $10.00. **Right:** Australian-made, embroidered on felt - $25.00. *Service:* Iwo Jima, China.

Sixth Marine Division
Australian-made, embroidered on twill using bright, silky threads, and mesh backing - $20.00. *Service:*

Guadalcanal, Eniwetok, Guam, Engebi, Saipan, Okinawa, North China, Occupation duties in Japan. This division's elements were widely scattered and often times, for extended periods of time, under the direction of other commands.

MARINE CORPS DIVISION NICKNAMES

First Division	*"Big One"- "Fighting First"*
Second Division	*"Silent Second"*
Third Division	*"Fighting Third"*
Fourth Division	*"Fighting Fourth"*
Fifth Division	*"Spearhead"*
Sixth Division	*"Striking Sixth"*

First Marine Amphibious Corps (I-MAC) Headquarters

Standard type - $25.00. *Service:* I-MAC Initially coordinated activities for the assault on Guadalcanal. It then coordinated the re-taking of the Solomon Islands. It assisted with the control of several campaigns prior to being re-designated as the Third Amphibious Corps in 1944.

Like the FMF PAC patch, I-MAC sub-units inserted their specific specialty design within the red diamond of the I-MAC patch. All of the sub-units are illustrated below. There are variations in the size of the five stars found on the I-MAC patches.

Parachute Battalions.

Standard type - $60.00. There were no combat parachute jumps conducted by the Marine Corps in WWII.

Aviation Engineers.

Standard type - $30.00.

Raider Battalions.

Standard type - $70.00. Variations in the skull details can be found. The Raiders were commando trained elite forces. They were developed to conduct reconnaissance operations, sabotage, operations, spearhead assaults, and other specialized duties. There were four battalions organized during the war.

Barrage Balloon Squadrons.

Standard type - $30.00.

Service and Supply.

Standard type: $30.00.

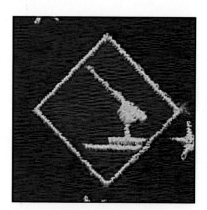

Defense Battalions.

Standard type - $30.00.

Artillery Battalions.

Standard type - $75.00 - $125.00. The artillery I-MAC patch is the most difficult of the standard series to find. There is another variation with thicker cannons.

I-MAC Service of Supply variations

Left: Full size, standard type (fully embroidered). **Right:** This is a "mini MAC" example - $20.00. The mini versions exist with all of the various I-MAC specialty symbols. The mini versions are embroidered on twill, and have a mesh backing. These are also heavily reproduced. Experience is about the only way to identify the reproductions from the originals. The mini Mac types average $20.00, but Raider, Paratroop, or Artillery examples command a higher price.

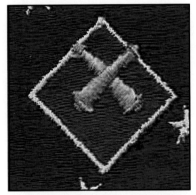

I-MAC Artillery Battalions with gold guns.

Rare, fully embroidered type. There is no absolute explanation for the gold gun variation. Some suggest it is an officer's version, and others claim it was worn by HQ personnel. Other theories are more obscure. I have yet to see any convincing support for these claims. In any case, the patch exists and was manufactured and used during WWII. It is a rare variation. Original gold gun designs have the cannons positioned in the upper portion of the red diamond, with the tips of the guns protruding to, and/or over, the white border. $175.00 - $225.00.

Reverse side of a "mini MAC" patch.

I-MAC Aviation Engineers patch with "ears"

Some I-MAC patches were manufactured with protruding corners at the top. These are more difficult to find than normal I-MAC types - $35.00.

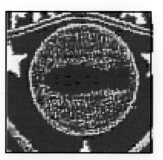

FMF-PAC Bomb Disposal Companies - $20.00.

Fleet Marine Force - Pacific (FMF-PAC) Headquarters

Standard type - $20.00. There are variations in the size of the three stars found on FMF patches. *Service:* FMF PAC was basically responsible for controlling the human and material resources dedicated to various Pacific island campaigns. It was also slated to function as the administrative command for multiple corps when the Japanese mainland was invaded. The surrender kept this from becoming a necessity. The FMF PAC design became the basis for all other FMF PAC sub-unit patches. These subordinate organizations simply inserted a symbol unique to their specialty within the gold circle of the FMF PAC patch. All the sub-unit designs are shown here:

FMF-PAC Dog Platoons - $30.00.

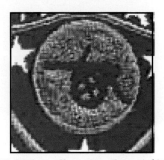

FMF-PAC Artillery Battalions - $20.00.

FMF-PAC Engineer Battalions - $20.00.

FMF-PAC Amphibious Tractor (amtracs) Battalions - $20.00.

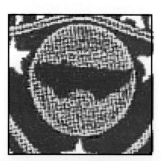

FMF-PAC Amphibious DUKW Companies - $20.00.

122

FMF-PAC Service of Supply (gold star) - $20.00.

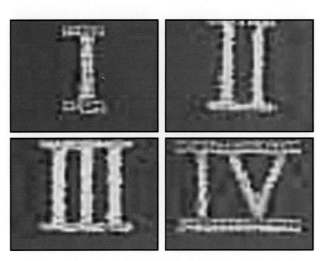

1st, 2nd, 3rd, and 4th Wing

White star - $20.00

1st Marine Air Wing (2nd style)

Standard type - $25.00. This is the 2nd style patch and it replaced the fuselage (shield) shaped design above. The headquarters version is identical except that the letters "PAC" replace the Roman numeral. The four subordinate wings were all numbered with Roman numerals (I, II, III, IV).

Headquarters Marine Air Wings - Pacific

Standard type $25.00. *Service:* Marine Air Wings - Pacific, was formed to coordinate the logistical and personnel activities of the Marine Air Wings in the pacific. The headquarters was stationed on Ewa. The headquarters patch is illustrated here, and the four subordinate Air Wings utilized the same design, but with the appropriate number of stars and Roman numeral reflecting the wing number. These patches were worn until the diamond shaped patch was adopted.

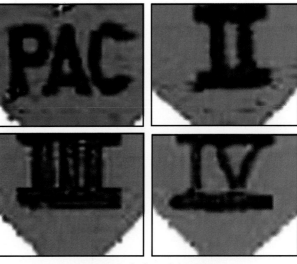

HQ, 2nd , 3rd, and 4th Wing

Fourth Marine Air Wing (old)

This is an embroidered on felt type - $150.00. A fully embroidered variation exists and commonly sells for $100.00+. This was an unofficial design worn by the Fourth Marine Base Defense Air Wing prior to the adoption of the diamond shaped patch illustrated earlier.

Herringbone USMC combat blouse

The illustrated blouse is typical of clothing worn in the field by Marine personnel. The inked "USMC" and the globe and anchor were common. Even in the inked insignia many variations in size and detail exist. It is not uncommon to find enlisted rank chevrons inked on the sleeves of Marine shirts as well.

Marine "novelty" jacket patch, 1930s - 40s era

Another nice example, embroidered on felt with mesh back - $45.00.

United States Navy

&

Coast Guard

The Navy and Coast Guard had very little in the way of official shoulder sleeve insignia other than rank and specialty designators. A number of unofficial types were adopted by aviation units, ships, submarines, and even installations. The sheer number of unofficial patches exceeds the scope of this book.

Navy "jumpers" and ranks insignia

Above are three examples of Navy jumpers and insignia. The jumper on the left has a Parachute Rigger 2nd Class rate on the left sleeve. Below that is a parachute qualification patch. And below that is a service stripe signifying 4-years of service. On the right breast is a gold "ruptured duck" patch, which represents that the wearer was honorably discharged. The jumper in the middle has an interesting Boatswains Mate 1st Class rate on the left sleeve. The eagle and stripes are applied to a dark blue felt. The background material for the patch has been shaped. This rate appears to have been tailor-made overseas. On the lower left cuff is a small shield and anchor.

This is the insignia for a Coast Guard Chief Petty Officer. It is believed to represent that the wearer, an ex-Coast Guard chief, was recalled for duty with the Navy and is now serving as a 1st class Petty Officer. The jumper on the right has the rate of an Aviation Ordinanceman 2nd Class, on the left sleeve. Just below the rate is a small white winged -"B", which means the wearer is a certified bombsight mechanic. On the right sleeve is the winged machine gun symbolizing that he is also a qualified aerial gunner. This jumper was tailor-made in the Philippines. Although the Navy did not have a good deal of unit insignia, like the Army and Marines, their uniforms are often adorned with special symbols like these. It was also common practice to have the inside of the jumper decorated with bright, colored stitching in various designs. This can usually be found on the inside of the cuffs and collar. The rates signifying the traditional seaman skills, like the boatswains mate, are worn on the right sleeve. All other skills are worn on the left sleeve.

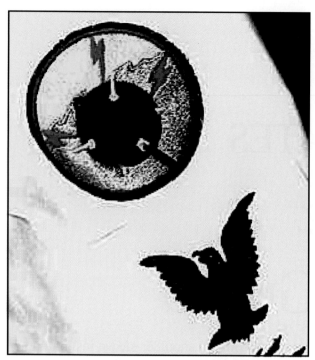

Navy Minecraft Personnel

This jumper belongs to a Radioman 1st Class, assigned to Minecraft. The Minecraft patch was authorized for enlisted personnel, only during their service on Minecraft. *Service:* Consisting of both minelayers and minesweepers, these craft served all over the world in both defensive and offensive roles. This is a standard patch - $20.00.

Navy Amphibious Forces variations

Left This is a U.S. made bullion on felt example with vendor's identification card still attached with a staple. The cheesecloth backing (white mesh) can be seen barely protruding around the edges of the patch - $60.00. The Amphibious Forces Atlantic Fleet Headquarters was located at Norfolk, Virginia. The vendor of this bullion design was also located in Norfolk, and the patch is primarily associated with personnel assigned to that headquarters. **Right** : This is the standard type - $8.00. This is one of the few unit shoulder sleeve insignia that was authorized for wear by the Navy. It could only be worn while actively assigned to the Amphibious Forces and was to be removed if the wearer was re-assigned. **Navy Amphibious Forces service:** These sailors were participants of every sig-

nificant amphibious assault that occurred throughout the war, both in the European and Pacific theaters.

The vendor's card stapled to the back of the Navy Amphibious Forces patch above.

The cheesecloth backing on this patch can be seen around the top of the card. Cheesecloth was used as backing on many WWII era patches. It is most commonly found on patches that are embroidered on felt or wool.

Navy Amphibious Craft crewman

Embroidered on felt - $15.00. Prior to other insignia being adopted for Amphibious personnel, this patch was worn by landing craft crews. It was worn on the lower sleeve of the blue jumper.

Navy Amphibious Forces – 1st style

Standard type - $50.00. This patch preceded the eagle and anchor design.

Patrol Torpedo Boat crewman

Standard type - $25.00. These patches were worn by enlisted crewman of "PT" boats. Like most Navy shoulder sleeve insignia, the patch could only be worn while actively serving with a qualifying unit. *Service:* The PT boats attacked enemy surface ships, conducted reconnaissance operations, rescues, special operations, minelaying, anti-submarine operations and a host of other assignments. PTs operated in the Pacific and European theaters.

Navy Construction Battalions (SeaBees or CBs)

Standard type - $15.00. This is probably the best known Navy shoulder unit insignia. *Service:* The Seabees were Navy Construction Battalions. The name is a derivative of the initials "C B", which appeared on their original distinctive insignia. The original patch was a small diamond in black or blue. Upon the square were the letters "CB" done in the contrasting color. The diamond patch was worn on the sleeve by construction battalion members that were not otherwise rated. The "CB" design can also be found as the "rate" symbol in petty officer rank patches. When the Seabees patch illustrated above was introduced, it became widely used. Many variations in color and detail exist. The Seabees served with incredible distinction in every area of the Pacific Theater of Operations.

They were responsible for building/repairing port facilities, installations, airfields, roads, water storage and treatment facilities, bridges, and anything else required. The Seabees frequently served as combat troops when necessary.

SEABEES variation

This SEABEES patch features the letters "CB" rather than "SEABEES". This particular patch appears to be a private purchase specimen and is a bit cruder than American, standard, fully embroidered types - $15.00.

Navy V-5 Program

Standard type with heavy green "snow" on the back - $50.00. *Service:* The V-5 Program was a method of combining college studies with flight training. It was a Naval Reserve project with close parallels to the Civilian Pilot Training (CPT) program. Graduates could earn commissions as Navy and Marine pilots. V-5 cadets held a unique rank between chief petty officer and warrant officer. Aside from the V-5 patch, which was worn on the cap as well as the sleeve, cadets wore a distinctive anchor cap badge on the visor cap. V-5 articles are quite scarce.

United States Maritime Service

Embroidered on canvas-like material $20.00. *Service:* The Maritime Service was responsible for training Merchant Marine personnel. During the war, merchant sailors risked and lost their lives in every theater. German submarines exacted a particularly dreadful toll on merchant vessels in the North Atlantic. The war simply could not have been won without these courageous sailors.

Ex-Navy Personnel

This patch was worn as a "combat patch", on the right shoulder of the Army uniform by soldiers who had prior wartime service in the Navy. It was not officially sanctioned.

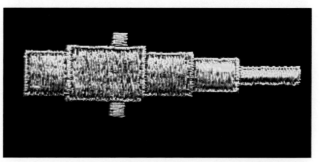

Gun Captain

This patch identified its owner as being in charge a ship's gun. In times of crisis, the gun captain was responsible for ensuring his assigned weapon was manned quickly and fired as directed.

Gun Pointer 1st Class

This patch was worn by Mr. Clarence Wells, of Oregon. Mr. Wells was a Gun Pointer assigned to one of the main forward turrets on the U.S.S. Pennsylvania. Mr. Wells was aboard when the ship was ravaged at Pearl Harbor and suffered a broken back during the attack. Mr. Wells was with the ship when it returned to action, and remained with her throughout the war.

Aerial Gunner

This patch identifies the wearer as a qualified aerial gunner. Aerial gunners manned defensive machine guns in aircraft like the Vindicator, Avenger, and SBD. The three previous patches are representative of the many distinguishing marks worn by Navy personnel. Some, like these, indicated that the wearer possessed a special skill or qualification. Similar patches were worn by sailors undergoing training in a particular skill. These patches would consist of a symbol representing the skill. For example, a sailor undergoing training to be Boatswain's Mate, would wear a square of cloth with crossed anchors embroidered on it. As the sailor makes rank, this symbol remains as the "rate" on his rank insignia. The rate is always immediately below the eagle on petty officer rank insignia.

Navy "E" (Excellence). Represents qualification by special crews or parties. The "E" was awarded for exceptional performance in gunnery or engineering. The gunnery "E" is white or blue. The engineering "E" is red. Subsequent awards are indicated by the addition of small bars below the "E". Marines are routinely assigned to larger warships for security purposes and to act as a landing force if necessary. To maximize the effectiveness of all personnel aboard ship, Marines were given additional responsibilities like operating and serving guns. Subsequently, Marines were eligible to wear the Navy "E" if the appropriate criteria was met. The Marine design is a red "E" on a green background

Submariner. Personnel assigned to duty on submarines often wore a white on blue or blue on white submarine patch at the cuff. This consists of a head-on silhouette of a submarine flanked on each side by stylized dolphins.

Marksmanship patch. Navy personnel who met necessary qualification standards were authorized to wear a marksmanship patch on the sleeve. This consists of a bulls-eye design on a square background.

United States Coast Guard

The Coast Guard wore uniforms identical to those of the navy. This shield device was worn on the cuff by all Coast Guard personnel. This shield was also made in silver and gold bullion thread. ***Service:*** Guard personnel performed myriad functions to include combat roles. Early in the war, Guardsmen patrolled American beaches on foot and with dogs when invasion seemed likely. They patrolled coastal waters in boats, ships, and aircraft in an anti-submarine role. Operating smaller boats and working ashore, Coast Guard personnel participated in every major invasion in the Pacific and European Theaters.

Coast Guard personnel at Elizabeth City, North Carolina, 1944

The Coast Guard shield can barely be seen on the left cuff of the male standing, and the male sitting on the left. Note the white shoulder stripes, which indicate that at least two of these Guardsmen are in training for seaman skills. A Coast Guard female (SPAR), is walking out of the barracks door. At far left is a woman in an unidentified uniform. Elizabeth City was the home of a Coast Guard air search and rescue station. The Marine air base at Cherry Point was close by. With a Navy dirigible installation on one side and a Navy air station on the other, it was a beehive of military activity.

SPAR, 1944

SPARS. The women's branch of the Coast Guard/Navy, had a distinctive patch design for wear on the collar. These consist of a white anchor superimposed on a blue, three bladed ship's propeller. These may be cut out types, or they may be embroidered on a disk of background material. SPARs also had a unique brassard for recruits, which was made of white silk with "*SPAR RECRUIT*" in dark blue letters.

Sailor and SPAR in white uniforms. Note the black shield on left cuff.

CLOTH ENLISTED RANK INSIGNIA

For centuries soldiers and sailors have worn symbols to identify their expertise and to indicate the extent of responsibility and authority delegated to them. As the military became more specialized and diverse, so have the symbols of recognition. By WWII, a fairly complicated system of identification was in use by all services. This section deals exclusively with the cloth insignia of the enlisted ranks. Although cloth examples do exist, officers normally wore metallic rank insignia.

Several variations of rank insignia were used during WWII. The Army's "technical" designator, indicating the wearer possessed a technical skill, was used in three grades and are unique to this period. They were Technician 3rd Grade (Staff Sergeant stripes with "T" added) Technician 4th Grade (Sergeant stripes with "T" added) Technician 5th Grade (Corporal stripes with "T" added).

The U.S. Army Air Forces had an unofficial chevron style which incorporated a winged propeller in the center of the chevron. These were most frequently used when the wearer qualified for a technician grade ("T" chevron).

Many of the WWII Navy chevrons (rates) were partially composed of bullion thread. Another interesting feature of WW II Navy rates is that many times they have the year, or place of manufacture sewn on the reverse. Others can be found with the initials of the maker and other odd details. At times, to break the monotony in the sewing mills, employees executed their own unique additions to these patches. The Navy rate, which features a stylized eagle above the chevrons, can occasionally be found with a brightly colored eye, or maybe a long wavy tongue. Other alterations were done in tailor shops at a sailor's request. Some of the most unique Navy rate variations were worn by Navy corpsmen assigned to the Marines. Navy rank insignia, from 3rd Class Petty Officer beyond, incorporate symbols representing the wearer's skill. These symbols are displayed immediately below the eagle ("crow" in navy-speak). Coast Guard personnel wore insignia essentially the same as the Navy.

The U.S. Marine Corps, U.S. Army, and U.S. Army Air Forces wore enlisted ranks on both sleeves. The U.S. Navy wore their rank patches on one sleeve only. Rates falling under the "Seaman" categories were worn on the right sleeve. All others rates were worn on the left sleeve.

Cloth rank insignia adds a colorful and interesting facet to any military collection. Even the most unique and unusual variations can be found at very reasonable prices. The most common materials and color combinations used by all branches are listed here.

Examples of the unofficial chevrons commonly used by Army Air Force personnel

Standard chevrons with a winged propeller added - $10.00. To further distinguish themselves from other GIs, some enlisted Air force personnel wore these unofficial chevrons. This is an example of an unofficial design that saw surprisingly wide-spread use. Apparently the Air Force assumed a tolerant position on these because they were worn in the United States as much as they were worn overseas. The winged propeller can be found in every Army enlisted rank, but they were intended for wear in lieu of the specialist ("T") chevrons, which came in only three grades.

U.S. ARMY / ARMY AIR FORCE:
Color combinations include:
Σ   Light brown stripes on khaki background
Σ   Light green stripes on khaki background.
Σ   Light pink stripes on khaki background.
Σ   Light gray stripes on dark blue / black background.
Σ   Medium green stripes on dark blue / black background.
Σ   Olive drab stripes on dark blue / black background.
Σ   White stripes on khaki background (China Burma India)
Σ   Black ink directly applied to sleeve

Construction Types:
Σ   Embroidered stripes on wool
Σ   Embroidered stripes on twill
Σ   Embroidered stripes on felt
Σ   Felt stripes applied to felt.
Σ   Felt stripes applied to twill
Σ   Felt stripes applied to wool
Σ   Stenciled directly to sleeve
Σ   Embroidered stripes on gabardine
Σ   Applied stripes on gabardine

Above: Examples of chevrons worn by the U.S. Army and Army Air Forces.

Lighter colored chevrons (khakis and pinks) were worn on the summer uniform. Darker colors were worn on the green uniform, fatigues, and battle dress. The many styles, materials, and colors make chevrons an interesting facet of WWII insignia in their own right.

Overseas stripes

Overseas stripes were worn on the lower left cuff. Each stripe represents 6 months of service in an overseas assignment. The stripes on the right, are made from a very fine metal wire.

Army service stripes. National Guard (6 years) on top, Federal (3 years) on bottom

Service stripes were awarded for every three years of service (term of enlistment at the time). They were worn diagonally on the lower left sleeve. Color variations can be found indicating Federal service (blue background) or National Guard service (buff background).

Wound stripes indicated wounds received during service in WWI. They were frequently seen on WWII era uniforms. These are inverted chevrons worn on the right lower sleeve. WWII wound stripes were embroidered like the overseas stripes shown previously.

WWI service as officer stripe. Enlisted ranks who had served as commissioned officers during WWI were authorized to wear a single stripe of dark green on both sleeves at the cuff. This applied to Warrant Officers as well.

Meritorious Unit Commendation, 4th award

Awarded to both American and Allied units for exceptionally meritorious conduct during combat operations. The unit must have been engaged in combat operations for a six-month period during 1944 and 1945. Soldiers who served in the unit for sixty-days or more, during the period that the award was earned, could display the patch on their uniform permanently. Others could wear the patch while assigned to the unit, but had to remove it upon leaving the unit. This patch consists of a yellow wreath on a khaki or olive drab square, and was worn on the lower right sleeve. Subsequent awards were indicated by the addition of a number within the wreath. A star was used to indicate five awards. These patches feature embroidered yellow numbers and wreath on a olive drab or khaki background. Bullion variations can also be found.

Examples of USMC chevrons

Left - Marine Gunnery Sergeant. Green felt stripes applied to khaki - $10.00. *Right, top:* Corporal. Green-felt chevrons applied to a red-felt base. *Right bottom:* This example has green stripes embroidered on a rigid red base material. Other variations include color printed types. It was not uncommon for Marines to draw or stamp stripes on their shirts in black ink.

133

U.S. MARINE CORPS:

Color combinations include:

Σ   Green stripes on red background
Σ   Green stripes on khaki background
Σ   Gold stripes on red background
Σ   Black ink directly applied directly to sleeve

Construction types:

Σ   Embroidered stripes on wool
Σ   Embroidered stripes on twill
Σ   Embroidered stripes on felt
Σ   Applied stripes on wool
Σ   Applied stripes on twill
Σ   Applied stripes on felt
Σ   Stenciled to shirt
Σ   Embroidered stripes on gabardine
Σ   Applied stripes on gabardine

Service stripes. These are diagonal stripes indicating four years service. Worn on lower sleeve.

Chief Petty Officer (Storekeeper)

This shows a Chief Petty Officer Storekeeper tunic with bullion insignia and gold chevrons. The service stripes are also gold. Gold represents twelve years of good conduct. Also note that the ribbons are directly embroidered on the jacket. The owner purchased this uniform from the Nudelman Brothers, Portland / Seattle outlet.

Examples of bullion Petty Officer insignia

(Above) Examples of bullion Navy petty officers rank insignia. ***Top row, left::*** Equipment Operator Chief Petty Officer. ***Right:*** Disbursing Clerk Chief Petty Officer. ***Bottom row, left::*** Engineman First Class. The gold stripes indicate twelve or more years with perfect conduct, ***Right::*** Machinist's Mate Chief Petty officer.

FOR U.S. NAVY / COAST GUARD:

Color combinations include:

Σ   Red stripes on dark blue background
Σ   Red stripes on dark green (assigned to Marine unit)
Σ   Blue stripes on dark green background
Σ   Blue stripes on white background
Σ   Blue stripes on khaki background
Σ   Gold stripes on dark blue background
Σ   Green stripes on khaki background (as signed to Marine unit)
Σ   Blue stripes on blue background
Σ   Black ink directly applied to sleeve
Σ   Blue stripes on gray and white striped background (For seersucker uniform)
Σ   Blue stripes on gray background

Construction types: Many Navy rank insignia incorporate bullion eagles and rate symbols. The use of bullion in Army, Army Air Force, and Marine rank insignia is rare. Other than this, the construction types are the same as for the other branches listed above.

Service stripes. These are long stripes worn diagonally on the lower sleeve. Each stripe represents four years of service. White on blue, blue on white, and red on blue are common. Gold service stripes indicate 12 or more years with perfect conduct.

Reverse side of marked Navy rate (1943)

Many Navy rates have markings on the reverse side. This is a manufacturing practice unique to WWII. Some were required as maker marks and others were done, on a whim, by the women operating the machines. Occasionally, unusual details can be found. Tongues may be added, eyes dotted, strange colors appear. It is my suspicion that many of these were the result of boredom and routine. Aside from dates, the variety of markings seems to be virtually endless. These would make an interesting collection in and of themselves. Navy rates are still very common and inexpensive. So far, there is no increase in value associated with marked examples.

Jumper of a "Fireman striker"

Branch marks. Navy jumpers will frequently be found with a stripe of white, blue, or red over the shoulder. The white or blue stripe represents the wearer as having a Seaman classification. Red represents the wearer as having a Fireman or other classification. Branch marks were worn by sailors that were not yet rated. Seaman wore the branch mark (white or blue depending on the uniform worn) on the right shoulder. All others wore a red branch mark on the left shoulder.

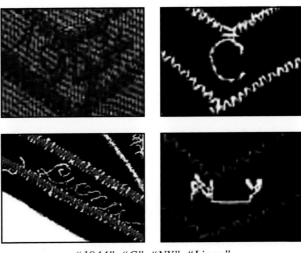

"1944", "C", "NY", "Liona"

Examples of the markings that can be found on the reverse side of Navy rates.

Example of searsucker pattern rate

The seersucker uniform was distinctive because of its vertical, gray stripes. Patches were made to match this uniform. These are not too frequently encountered. Other Navy uniforms included tan, black, blue, white, and green.

Examples of U.S. Navy specialty marks in Marine Corps colors

Top row: Left - Machinist's mate *Right* - Ordinanceman *Bottom Row: Left* Torpedoman. This patch is in the original wrapper with a New York Emblem Corporation label. *Right* - Avaiation Ordinanceman. $8.00 each. Many Navy personnel were assigned to Marine units. During these assignments, sailors could wear Marine uniforms. Consequently, some Navy insignia had to be manufactured in colors that would match the green Marine tunic. That was the official purpose for these odd insignia. Additionally, marines assigned to ships were often cross-trained to perform some critical functions in

times of emergency. Marines learned to operate small guns, to fight fires, and other tasks. Consequently, Marines sometimes wore a Navy "specialty patch" symbolizing their additional skill.

Navy Corpsman 3rd class, assigned to Marines

Historically, the Navy has supplied combat medics (corpsman) to Marine Corps combat units. The sailors assigned to Marine units are entitled to wear the Marine Corps uniform. In these cases the Navy rank insignia is modified in color to coordinate with the Marine tunic. Navy rates in Marine colors can also be found with red chevrons applied to a forest green background material. During WWII, many Navy personnel were assigned to Marine units. Frequently, Navy Construction Battalion sailors (SeaBees) were attached to amphibious Marine engineer units. These rates normally have a construction related specialty symbol like heavy equipment operator, machinist, carpenter, electrician, and so on. Navy rates in Marine colors are relatively difficult to find. For this corpsman example - $45.00.

The Navy and Coast Guard had several rates of their own that were unique to the war years. These are known as the "letter rates". Due to the sudden wartime demand for experienced personnel, certain civilians with critically needed expertise were gathered. These occupational specialties were given letter designations. These letters were applied to the rank patches and were considered actual rates. All of these variations will have a diamond shape surrounding the letter. These include the letters: "I" (International Business Machines), "C" (Classification Interviewers), "A" (Athletic Instructors), "G" (Gunnery Instructors), "W" (Welfare), "T" (Teachers), "P" (Photographers), "V" (Transport Airmen), "M" (Mail Clerks), "O" (Material Inspectors), "R" (Recruiter) and "S" (Shore Patrol).

*Examples of Navy "diamond" rates: From left to right:
(T)eacher, (P)hotographer, and (W)elfare*

AUTHENTICITY
IDENTIFYING REPRODUCTIONS

This is merely a summary of techniques for determining authenticity of WWII patches. Additional facts and examples are included liberally throughout the book to reinforce the reader's understanding.

Some confusion exists with the terms "reproduction" and "current". Improper use of these terms can create a less than amiable conversation between a buyer and seller. We will use the 1st Infantry Division patch as an example. This patch has been worn from WWI to the Persian Gulf. A 1st Division patch issued in the 1990's, is not a reproduction. It is merely a current issue patch. Current patches are worth markedly less than a WWI or WWII issue patch.

A "reproduction" is a newer rendition of a patch that was active during a specific period(s) in the past, and is represented as being from that period. For example, the Marine Londonderry Detachment patch was specific to WWII. It was not worn prior to the war and it has not been worn since. Therefore, a more recently manufactured Londonderry Detachment patch is a reproduction. Reproductions have been manufactured for decades. Many WWI designs were reproduced in the 1940's. This is important to know because many reproductions are old. They are not easy to detect based on appearance.

Reproductions are often called "collector copies" or "repros" by reputable dealers. This is to ensure that prospective buyers know that the item listed is a counterfeit. Useful perhaps, to fill holes in a display until an authentic example can be found. Sadly, and more often than not, this distinction is not made. These patches are wrongly and deliberately represented as authentic, for authentic prices. The unwary buyer may never know otherwise. Even reputable dealers mistake reproductions for authentic pieces on occasion.

For these reasons the collector should become intimately familiar with the information in this book. It is cheap insurance that will pay enormous dividends if adhered to. There are a number of ways to detect reproduction patches and patches that are of current manufacture. For the purposes of this book, "current" refers to insignia manufactured after the Korean War. Many of the insignia worn during the Korean War were surplus from WWII, and are therefore genuine. Patches made during the early 1950's are usually identical in every respect to those made in the 1940's and command comparable prices.

The Korean war resulted in many theater-made or overseas- (Asian) made variations. These include machine-embroidered, hand-embroidered, and combinations of bullion and tinsel. Some bullion and embroidered types have attached tabs and scrolls with "KOREA" on them. Korean-made bullion variations can occasionally be identified by the material and workmanship. But in most cases, the differences are so subtle that no accurate assessment can be made by the average collector. The level of knowledge required to discern between some Korean types and some WWII types is far beyond the capabilities of a single book. Knowing what units served in Korea will help. It is also recommended that collectors study illustrated (reputable) patch publications and dealer lists. Eventually the collector will recognize types and styles of variations that are known to be unique to Korea. in any case, as was previously mentioned, these Korean variants are very desirable and command comparable prices. Collectors should not be too preoccupied with whether or not a quality patch is WWII or Korea vintage.

Few of the charactcristics listed here for identifying genuine insignia, when considered individually, are conclusive. But WWII patches will *always* have some of these, and when considered collectively, the buyer can be fairly certain that he or she has acquired a "good" piece. On the other hand, some of the characteristics of a currently manufactured patch *always* indicate that the patch is new or reproduction. By utilizing these tips, the collector can make sound and educated purchases.

SUMMARY OF CHARACTERISTICS - WWII FACTORY-EMBROIDERED PATCHES.

SNOW:

A characteristic commonly found in machine embroidered WWII patches is "snow" on the reverse (back) side. Snow is usually white, but may be green, black, and on rare occasions, other colors. Snow varies in density and may at times actually make it difficult, or impossible to recognize what the front of the patch looks like. There are numerous examples illustrated throughout this book.

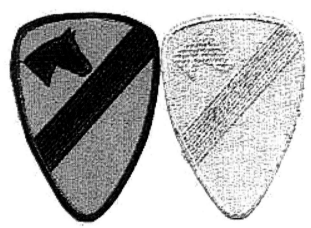

When you examine the reverse sides, the WWII patch is covered with "snow".

Since the introduction of polyester, nylon and other synthetics, colored thread has become less expensive. It is no longer necessary to switch to a white bobbin when working on the reverse side of a patch. The commercial embroidering process has also been greatly simplified eliminating unnecessary mechanical movements and processes. Consequently, in current manufacturing, if the front of the design is to be yellow and green, yellow and green will be the primary colors on the reverse as well. A few specks of white thread may be present, but the reverse will normally appear the same as the front, except not quite as "finished' or "focused" looking. Synthetic thread was not used in patches during WWII. Patches of the period were produced from materials like cotton, wool, rayon and silk. Many current and reproduction patches are manufactured with synthetic threads. Despite the efforts of many manufacturers in duplicating the precise appearance of a WWII vintage insignia, the use of nylon thread is a dead giveaway of a fake.

The 1st Cavalry patch on the left is new. The patch on the right is WWII vintage.

WWII patches.

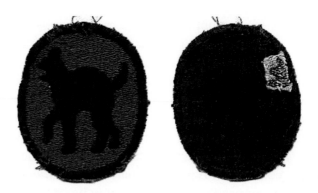

Left: *81st Division patch.* Right: *Same patch in reverse, showing heavy concentration of black snow.*

Even when the body of a WWII patch is not densely covered with snow, the high points of the edge and details will usually have a heavy concentration.

Same patches in reverse. Note the white, brown and green "snow"

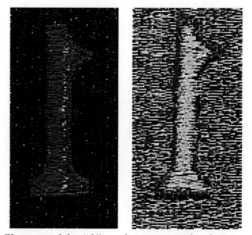

Left: *Close-up of the "1" on the reverse side of a current 1st Division patch. Note the almost total absence of snow.* Right: *Close-up of the "1" on the reverse side of a WWII 1st Division patch. Note the heavy concentration of white snow.*

Snow is one of the quickest and most reliable methods of detecting reproduction designs. A factory embroidered patch with no "snow" on the back, which is represented as being WWII vintage, should trigger a red-flag to the prospective buyer.

BURN TEST:

Although I do not recommend this, it is possible to discern between many natural fibers like cotton and rayon, and synthetics like nylon and polyester by the way they burn. Some collectors try to find a loose thread from a patch in question and light it with a lighter or match. Cotton tends to burn like paper; uniformly and with a predictable speed. Synthetics will melt like plastic and the flame tends to behave somewhat erratically. The remaining end of a burned synthetic thread will be shiny black, melted and hard. The end of a burned cotton thread will assume a dark brown color and generally remains pliable and soft. There is reportedly a difference in the odor as well, but I have never been able to discern from the odor with any degree of reliability.

ULTRAVIOLET LIGHT TEST:
(Often times, improperly referred to as the blacklight test).

White portions of natural materials like silk, linen, cotton, rayon and wool do not react to UV light. White portions of synthetic materials do. By passing the patch under a UV lamp, the white nylon will react by glowing brightly. You should try this first at home by using a patch you know has white nylon thread, and one with cotton. The UV lamp is still just that, a lamp. So, even cotton designs will brighten a bit. But the nylon will react like neon. Once you have seen the difference, there will be no doubt whatsoever what the nylon reaction looks like. And you can use it with confidence from that point on. Don't allow self-proclaimed experts to convince you that there are lots of exceptions to this rule. There aren't. If the patch reacts to UV light, it isn't WWII vintage. The lamp utilized by the author is about the size of a mini cassette recorder. It operates on four AA batteries. It fits in the pocket and can be carried to gun shows, flea markets, antique shops, and anyplace else where patches may be found. The rest of the time it fits nicely in the glove box of a car. It's always handy if needed.

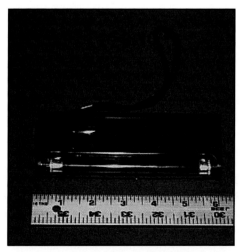

Pocket-size Ultraviolet light

In 1996, I found a very rare Nazi armband in an antique store. It was a combination of embroidery and fine bullion on a base piece of material. It was aged and worn. Some fading was present in spots. There were a couple minor moth nips in it as well. The price was substantial, but its worth was much more substantial. The author agonized about buying it for quite some time. It was examined and re-examined at length. The dealer had a plausible and detailed explanation of provenance. The author was pretty thoroughly convinced that it was "good". Discretion finally took hold and the author left with the intent to return in a week or so with my UV lamp. Upon my return, the armband was examined using the UV lamp. It glowed from one end to the other. There were white nylon threads throughout the design. It was the best reproduction that I have ever seen, and was masterfully aged. The UV lamp paid for itself, ten times over, on that purchase alone!

Not all reproductions are made with nylon thread. But any patch with nylon thread is definitely of newer manufacture.

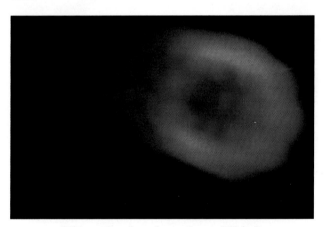

White nylon thread reacting to UV light

Above: This photo shows a reproduction 9th Airborne patch reacting to ultraviolet light. This particular patch was marked $50.00 at a collector show. The lamp cost less than that. If a patch reacts to UV light, it can immediately be dismissed as being of recent manufacture. To the left of the glow is a WWII 9th Airborne patch with white cotton thread. It does not react to the UV light and is invisible here.

Many patches from WWI to WWII incorporate a mesh backing. This is particularly true of the 1920's - 1930's designs. Therefore, many reproductions are executed with mesh backing as well. Many of these reproductions use cotton thread in the patch, but the mesh is often made from nylons and will react to the UV light, thus exposing them as counterfeit.

MERROWED EDGES:

Merrowed edges began to replace other styles in the mid-1960s. The merrowed edge is a heavy, complex stitch applied to the edges of a patch to prevent fraying. These patches are distinctive due to the very pronounced edge, the small chain stitch on the inside of the front edge, and the tire-tread design found on the reverse edge. Merrowed patches frequently have a "pigtail" of thread still attached to the edge on the reverse side. This is frequently held down with a small piece of tape or other sticky substance. One variation of the 506th Parachute Infantry Regiment patch was produced with a border very much resembling the merrowed edge. With that exception, if a patch has a merrowed edge, it was produced long after WWII.

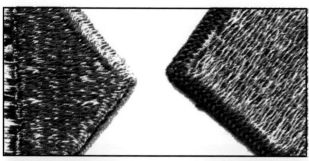

Top left: *WWI Cut-edge patch (reverse)*. Top right: *current merrowed edge patch (reverse)*. Bottom left: *WWII cut edge patch (front)*. Bottom right: *current merrowed edge patch (front)*.

EVIDENCE OF USE:

I have always preferred patches that are in good, but used condition. Evidence of use and removal from a uniform helps to confirm authenticity. Collectors who seek only mint, pristine examples will not benefit from this section. There are several indicators of a patch having been formerly worn. The most obvious is the presence of thread protruding from the edge. Many times when a patch is cut from a uniform, several strands of thread will remain. Unless the owner makes a deliberate attempt to pull each one out, these strands will remain forever. An example of this is the French Forces Training in America patch, which is illustrated on page 140. The severed khaki threads that once bound the patch to a uniform can be seen all the way around the perimeter of the patch.

Another indicator is holding the patch between the eye and a bright light. Often times, the light will shine through the holes left by a sewing needle around the perimeter of the patch.

Yet another clue is a wavy appearance around the edge of a patch. Sometimes, if the patch was sewn tightly, the taut threads will leave a pattern of indentations all around the patch.

Marine Detachment Londonderry. Which patch would you buy?

Marine Detachment Londonderry in reverse

If you were faced with purchasing one of these patches, which would you select? The patch on the right has a heavy presence of snow, which is a characteristic of WWII patches. Also note the lines visible around the edge, which are indentations from thread having bound it tightly to a uniform at one time. A clue can be found by analyzing the front picture. These two observations suggest strongly that the patch on the right is a genuine piece. The patch on the left is a reproduction.

BULLION:

WWII bullion patches are found in combinations of material. Metallic threads of silver, gold, or both may be used. Some designs incorporate tinsels, sequins and other metallic devices. Most of the metal threads used during WWII are vulnerable to patina, which is the result of natu-

142

ral oxidation processes. Bullion patches purported to be WWII, should exhibit some patina and discoloration. After more than fifty years, even patches that were never worn will show some indications of age. Occasionally, a bullion patch can be found that has been stored properly and appears bright, shiny and new. None of the characteristics listed here are absolute. But when considered collectively they provide a very good general rule of thumb.

There are thousands of bullion patches flooding the market from Pakistan, Thailand, Singapore and other locations. Although attractive, they are usually more simplistic and uniform in appearance. They are also somewhat more organized looking on the reverse. Period designs were often hand-made. Current designs are mass produced, and appear that way. Current metallic threads do not resemble the high-quality bullions of the 1940's and 50's. In most cases, the threads are not metal and have a plastic appearance when viewed closely. Be wary of clean, shiny, new-looking pieces. Many of the reproductions flooding the market recently include Army Air Forces, Army divisions and Armor Division patch designs. In the Army Air Force section is a vintage, bullion 10th Army Air Force patch. This patch was kept in a cigar box from the time it was purchased in India (1944), until October 1997. It was never worn, seldom handled, and well protected from the elements. It is about as mint as they come. Despite this, it shows age. The materials and craftsmanship are beautiful, but imperfect. Bullion designs that are precisely manufactured, and look brand new, probably are brand new. Copper threads have been used to reproduce WWII bullion designs since the 1950s. Despite many claims to the contrary, copper was not a common component of WWII era patches. Examples of copper reproductions can be found in the Army Air Force section.

QUALITY:

Quality of manufacture can be another indicator. Although some reproductions are high-quality designs, others are very cheaply executed. These will often be embroidered on twill types. They frequently have merrowed edges and will often have a waxy substance on the reverse. After a little experience in collecting, the poor quality reproductions will be conspicuously obvious.

Tank Destroyer Forces patches.

The design on the top is original. The lower design is a reproduction. Note the thick, full thread details on the top patch. The tank track detail is also much more precise. Of particular importance is the black border (edge). The edge on the top patch is thickly and completely covered with black thread. The edge of the patch on the bottom is sparsely covered, and there are gaps where the yellowish underlay is visible. This economy of thread is completely uncharacteristic of older patches. The workmanship alone identifies this patch as a reproduction. Also note the color itself. The Tank Destroyer colors are orange and black. This yellow example is an improper shade. Most four-wheel Tank Destroyer patches incorporate red details in the tongue area, which this patch does not have. Genuine four, six and eight-wheel variations can be found.

PROVENANCE:

Provenance is the best guarantee of authenticity. Obtaining the item from a veteran is the best reassurance the collector can have. I suggest obtaining some history from the veteran to include name, serial number, unit(s), service dates, duties, rank, service locations and a summary of experiences if possible.

Documentation of a particular item's history always enhances the value. A picture of the veteran wearing the patch and any other related bits and pieces make a great display. Additionally, a group of items which are attributable to a specific person, are always more desirable than an unattributed group.

MOTHING:

Moth nips and damage are certainly indicative of some age, but like any other collectible, condition has a direct association to value.

PRICING:

When you are at a show or antique store where the proprietor or dealer apparently has some knowledge of militaria, and you find an item which is offered for a fraction of its worth, beware. Occasionally one can find a true bargain. Sometimes, a rare or unusual item cannot be located and identified by the dealer from the general reference books commonly available. Once in a while a true treasure slips by at a give-away price. But, as a rule, if the price is too good to be true...

Knowledge is everything. If you study your hobby relentlessly you will find more and more incredible buys. That is the very purpose of this book. To provide the patch collector with the ability to recognize the rare pieces and the valuable variations which are seldom, if ever, illustrated in the reference books used by most retailers. But, without knowledge, you can waste an incredible amount of money buying junk. The best investment any collector can make is gaining knowledge of the subject matter.

AVAILABILITY:

A buyer should beware if a dealer has an abundance of rare material. This should be qualified to mean gun show, military show, and flea market tables that are covered with items that are rarely encountered. This is particularly true when the dealer has several identical copies of a rare design or variation. This should be an instantaneous "red flag" to the buyer. Occasionally a cache of rare items is discovered or liquidated by a collector, but this is more unique to reputable dealers than it is to weekend flea market types.

WAXY-BACKS AND SIZING:

Many patches of newer manufacture have a waxy substance applied to the reverse. This is not a characteristic of WWII insignia. Do not confuse this with remnants of glue. Many collectors glue patches to scrapbooks, boards and material for display purposes. When removed from the boards, some of this glue will inevitably remain. Glue remnants however, will normally be accompanied by paper, cloth, cardboard, or other evidence of prior mounting. Glue remnants will not be uniformly present across the reverse of the patch. The waxy substance will be uniformly applied.

This substance becomes tacky when heated and helps to secure the patch to a uniform. This is a relatively recent innovation on patches.

Another opaque substance can be found on patches including earlier designs. This substance is commonly referred to as "sizing". It is a stiffening agent that is sprayed or brushed onto material. In the case of patches, it usually can be found on the reverse edges to prevent fraying, and across the reverse side to make the patch more rigid and crisp. Sometimes the only evidence of sizing is tiny glitters visible when the reverse side is scrutinized very closely. These glitters almost appear to be tiny bits of glass sparkling between the threads. Sizing did not become a common feature on patches until the 1950's. Most patches with sizing on the back are post-WWII.

MISCELLANEOUS:

Other indicators include soiling, fading from sustained exposure to sunlight, and varying degrees of damage to the edge, which can be caused if a patch is ripped from a uniform. Remember, unless a patch is scarce, damaged examples should be avoided. Like any other collectable, condition has a very heavy influence on value.

Critical point: Rare patches *rarely* surface. This is incredibly simple, but incredibly difficult to keep in mind. A phenomenon that I have witnessed over and over again, is the appearance of several identical rare patches at about the same time. This is a frequent occurrence on internet auctions. If you see an exceptionally rare type surface at an auction or on a dealer list, check as many other sites as you can. If you see one of these "ultra rare" patches on eBay, and then you find one on Yahoo, and then you see one listed in so and so's list, you must recognize the likelihood that someone just had a batch made. For example, this occurred with the Red Ball Express patch around 1998 / 1999. These patches were painstakingly made to appear exactly like the French made originals. Very recent examples include the Womens Army Service Pilot (WASP) patch, airborne tabs for the 80th Division patch, airborne tabs in the white on red configuration, Ranger tabs in the white on red configuration, armored battalion triangles, AVG leather patches, and countless others. Rare patches *rarely* surface. If every site has one, the red flags should go up. Use good judgment, do your homework, and apply logic, knowledge and common sense in making your decision.

144

TERMS & ABBREVIATIONS

Every skill or interest results in a vocabulary of "insider" jargon and military collecting is no different. This is particularly true with people who produce lists of items. Some dealers or auction house lists contain thousands of pieces that need to be accurately described to ensure that customers know precisely what it is they are purchasing. The time involved in preparing a list can be drastically reduced if some common and easily understood abbreviations are used. Understanding these abbreviations is critical to the collector as they will offer evidence of age, quality, worth and scarcity. Some abbreviations may suggest the origin of the piece and its condition. Although exceptions certainly exist, the following definitions and explanations will provide a great foundation of understanding, and should assist the collector in selecting desired items from amongst other pieces.

WWII had a devastating effect on the commerce and economies of many foreign nations. The traditional means of generating income were in many cases, no longer available to the native populations. As an alternative, despite the shortage of materials created by the war, many enterprising individuals managed to manufacture and sell attractive insignia to American forces overseas. In many cases this was the only potential for families to generate income. This practice continued for some time after the war because U.S. forces remained in several overseas locations for occupation duties. These theater-made versions often have a value that far exceeds the value of the standard American embroidered type. Theater-made patches are often beautifully hand-crafted in multiple textiles, metals and tinsels. They may be incredibly detailed, or crude and simplistic. Regardless, in many instances they are truly one-of-a-kind creations. Consequently, dealers and collectors make reference when possible as to the location of manufacture, or at least that the patch or insignia is theater made. Without some experience it is usually impossible to determine the origin of a theater-made patch based solely on its construction. However, by determining the service locations of the unit the patch represents, it is possible to combine that information with the type of construction and conclude with some certainty where it was produced. For example: a bullion China Burma India patch is probably not an Italian bullion design. Conversely, a bullion 88th Infantry Division patch was probably not produced in China, Burma, or India since the 88th spent its entire wartime service in Italy and Trieste, remaining there for occupation after the war. A bullion 8th Army Air Force patch is probably English made considering that the 8th AAF arrived in England in 1942, and remained there until 1945. While there are no absolute guarantees aside from hallmarks and established provenance, logic is the key. The author included countries that were significant sources of theater made insignia below. These are frequently referred to in lists and publications. Also included are the major construction types for insignia that are known to have originated from each country. These are *common* construction types for those countries and there are exceptions for each. But, armed with this information and the areas of service for each unit, the collector can make a reasonable assumption, in most cases, where the patch originated. The bottom line though, is as long as the patch is original, the precise location of origin, while nice to know, is somewhat incidental.

American made – For the wartime years, the predominant manufacturing style in America was the fully embroidered type. Patches were made however, with embroidered designs on muslin, canvas, wool, felt, twill, and other materials. Leather patches were also produced and usually consisted of details either decaled or silk screened onto a leather base. American made insignia are characterized by their high-quality, uniform, machined appearance. Foreign types often have a more crude, handmade, individualistic appearance.

Left: *WWII types in olive drab.* Right: *Post-1957 in army green.*

Left: *American made.* Right: *Theater made.*

Army Green - Refers to the army uniform color after 1957. When the uniform color changed, so did the patch designs that incorporated the uniform color in the background or around the edges. Army green is a very dark, deep shade. Almost all patches that incorporate the army green color are post-Korea (1957 or later) manufacture.

Ultra rare Armored Recon patch with army green border - 1960s

Attached tab - Many patches like the 10th Mountain and all airborne divisions incorporate a tab as part of their design. When the tab and patch are manufactured as one piece, it is considered to be an "attached" or "integral" tab design.

Integral tabs

Normally, the excess material between the tab and patch is removed.

Australian made - Australia was a major R&R location for American troops in the pacific. As a result, numerous shops catered to GIs with tailoring services and the manufacture and sale of private-purchase uniforms and insignia. Australian made patches include fully embroidered, embroidered on felt or wool, bevo-like materials, silk and others.

Bevo - Refers to a particular weave and appearance. The word is a derivative of the business name - Bandfabrik Ewald Vorsteher, one of the predominant German insignia manufacturers, who utilized this distinctive weave to produce their insignia. Many Dealers and collectors refer to any patch with a flat, finely woven appearance as bevo. Many marine patches originating from Australia, for example, were done in a bevo-like weave, but are not genuine bevo examples. True bevo patches are very distinctive and are most commonly associated with European manufacturers. Bevo patches are highly sought after and almost always command premium prices.

Reverse side of a genuine, German made bevo armor patch. The tab is not bevo.

Close-up of bevo Supreme Headquarters Allied Powers Europe (SHAPE) patch.

Although this is a post-war insignia it is included to illustrate the distinctive appearance of a German made bevo patch. Note the incredibly fine weave and pebbled texture. SHAPE patches are somewhat scarce - $50.00.

Blacklight – Many dealers refer to a patch as having "passed the blacklight test". This is a declaration that the patch is all natural fiber threads and is a genuine WWII piece. Unfortunately, blacklights don't work. *Ultraviolet* light will cause a reaction with white synthetic thread causing the white to glow brilliantly. Synthetics were not used in patches during WWII. Therefore, if the patch reacts, it is post-WWII manufacture. A couple years ago, a lengthy dissertation appeared in a publication produced by a military insignia collectors periodical. The article essentially tried to suggest in convoluted, scientific terms, that WWII vintage patches could be wrongly discarded as fakes because of misinterpreted UV light reactions. The author went on to list a number of scenarios that could result in UV light reaction on authentic patches. One scenario involved synthetic dust or fiber debris becoming attached to the patch in storage or inadvertent contact with other material. Another scenario included having a vintage uniform dry cleaned and the chemicals from the dry cleaning process reacting to UV light. Yet another theory was that glue residue, remaining on a patch that had been glued to a display at one time, may have chemicals that react to UV light. In any of these cases, the collector would see random, irregular spots of reaction. It would be obvious that some foreign substance was the cause, and this should be of no consequence to the collector. If a patch has white synthetic threads in the design, *all* of the white portion will react brilliantly and uniformly. This is what the collector needs to be wary of. If this occurs, without exception, the patch is not WWII vintage

My pocket-size ultraviolet lamp

Top: Identifies the wearer as acting in capacity as a sergeant. **Bottom:** This brassard has a Combat Leadership Training patch displayed. This patch was introduced in the 1940s. Each brassard has three rows of snap closures for size adjustment. The snaps are marked "RAU KLIKIT".

Bullion - Twisted gold or silver metallic thread. Bullion designs often incorporate metallic tinsels and sequins as well. Some patches can be found with bullion, tinsel, sequins and metal devices in the same design.

This 6"x2" lamp also has a white light in one end, which is helpful. This lamp is primarily designed for law enforcement functions. However, I ordered one for evaluation and it proved incredibly convenient and effective. It has paid for itself literally hundreds of times. A catalogue featuring this and similar lamps can be obtained at the following address:

Lynn Peavey Company
P.O. Box 14100
Lenexa, Kansas 66285-4100

Brassard – A Brassard is an armband normally made of silk, cloth, or nylon. Brassards were worn with some frequency during WWII, and indicated that the wearer was performing some special purpose. Military Policemen wore brassards with "MP" on them. Shore Patrolmen wore "SP". Airborne and invasion forces often wore brassards displaying the American flag. Another purpose of a brassard was identifying an individual who was temporarily acting in the capacity of an advanced rank. This is a common practice in training environments where students are appointed to fill leadership roles on a rotating or trial basis. Numerous brassards can be found with different titles, patches, and recognitions. Brassards usually have a lacing system or snaps for size adjustment.

Indian made CBI patch

Above: China Burma India patch. The silver stripes, star, and sun are bullion. Silver sequins have also been incorporated. The basketweave red embroidery is typical of pieces originating from India. **Below:** American made bullion rate for a Chief Petty Officer. Bullion Navy rates were usually handmade.

Set of Combat Leadership Training brassards

Chief Petty Officer's rate

Bullion depiction of the Taj Mahal Agra. This pillow case was made in India - 1944.

Canvas / Muslin - These materials were frequently used for the base fabric or backing of patches. These materials were widely used. Canvas is a coarse weave while muslin is a very fine cotton weave.

Canvas and muslin backed patches.

Kiska Task Force patch printed on canvas.

Cased - Means that the piece is accompanied by the container it was issued in. This can enhance the value to varying degrees. A cased piece is more desirable than an otherwise identical, un-cased piece.

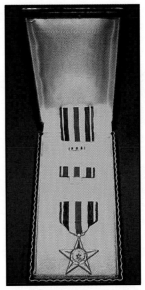

Cased Silver Star Medal

This is an example off a "cased" decoration. It comes in the original box and includes the ribbon bar, lapel bar, and extra material as issued.

CB - Clutch-Back. This generally indicates WWII - current manufacture. Clutch back insignia have pins on the reverse, designed to penetrate clothing. To keep the insignia secured, there are small metal or plastic caps. The caps grasp the pins by friction.

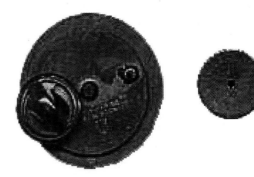

Clutch back enlisted man's disc

Left: Reverse side of an enlisted man's disc worn on the lapel/collar. The cap is on the left side pin and the right side pin is exposed. At the lower center of the disc, barely visible, is the Meyer Insignia Company hallmark consisting of a shield and writing. **Right:** This is a clutch back cap showing the hole where the pin is inserted.

Chenille - Is a method of embroidery which results in a coarse, looped appearance similar to a carpet. Athletic achievement letters and school logos are frequently done in chenille and are applied to the "letterman's" jacket. Many Army Air Force squadron insignia were produced in chenille.

Chenille 30th Infantry Regiment jacket patch (1939).

CBI Theater made - China Burma India (CBI) Myriad uniform and patch variations originated from the CBI area during and after the war. Major construction types include leather, silk, hand-embroidered, bullion, printed and twisted chord. Some designs incorporate tinsels and metal devices. Numerous examples are shown throughout this book.

Collector copy: This is another term for reproduction patch. During the 1940s, companies like the Patch King, who produced patches for the military, began marketing patches to collectors as well. Copies of rare WWII designs as well as most of the WWI designs, were produced for collectors. Despite being reproductions, they are now 55 years old. Currently, several companies make copies of WWI, WWII, Korean, and Vietnam patches for collectors. These are usually factory machine embroidered and do not exhibit the quality characteristics of older patches. All of these fall into the collector copy category.

Condition descriptions: Vary to some degree from dealer to dealer, but generally as follows:

Mint = Virtually good as new, perfect, unused condition. Some natural aging may be present and does not necessarily detract from a mint classification.

XF = Extra Fine, slightly less than mint, but very nice.

VF = Very Fine, slightly less than extra fine.

Excellent = Extra Fine - Very Fine

F = Fine, very good condition

Good = a nice representative piece, easily recognizable. May have some wear / use evident.

Fair = Still identifiable, worn but generally intact. A representative piece.

Poor = Worn, weathered, tattered, broken, missing pieces etc. Will usually be accompanied by some explana-

tion. For the purposes of American shoulder sleeve insignia, seldom is this condition worth consideration.

Cotton – Although synthetics were being experimented with prior to the war, most standard WWII patches were made from cotton thread. White cotton does not react to ultraviolet (UV) light. White synthetic threads will react like neon if exposed to UV light. If a patch is exposed to UV light and it glows intensely, it is almost certainly not a WWII insignia.

Crazed - This refers to leather pieces that have developed cracking (spider-webs) in the paint, decal, or leather itself.

Heavily "crazed" leather patch. Leather 15th AAF patches are rare.

Cut edges - This is a term often used to identify a patch as being WWII / Korean vintage. Patches of these periods will have a trace of the material they were cut from along the edge. This material is usually olive drab or khaki, but blue, black and other colors can be found. Due to use and age, some fraying is usually present. In an attempt to discourage fraying, cut-edge patches have a border of thread that is applied perpendicular to the threads in the body of the patch. This creates a raised rim around the perimeter of the patch. A cut-edge does not constitute proof that a patch was produced in the 1940s-1950s. Cut-edge patches were produced long after that.

  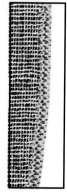

Left: *Khaki cut-edge, characteristic of WWII era manufacture.*
Middle: *Front edge of a merrowed patch. Note the chain-link stitch on the inside of the yellow edge.* **Right:** *Back edge of a merrowed patch. Note the distinctive tire-tread design.*

150

DI's - Distinctive Insignia, also referred to as crests. These are small metal, cloth, ribbon, or plastic unit badges. No army in the world has developed a greater passion for these insignia than the U.S. Army. Thousands of DIs exist. Normally DIs are approved for units of regimental size. Some DIs have been designed and worn by battalions and companies. WWII also saw the manufacture and use of crests bearing the patch designs of armies, corps, divisions, commands, air forces and other units. Most DIs are metal, but DIs may also appear as ribbons sewn to shoulder straps (like the one worn by the 4th Infantry Regiment), embroidered designs sewn to the uniform, or embroidered designs sewn to loops which are slid or snapped onto the shoulder straps.

English made - The lengthy presence of American forces in England resulted in thousands of English-made, private purchase uniforms and insignia. Primary construction types include machine embroidered on felt, hand-embroidered on felt, bullion on felt, printed, leather and silk. Many metal insignias were also produced in England.

Error design: These are variations of patches resulting from a mistake in the manufacturing process. These include reversed colors, incorrect shapes, added or missing details, and so forth. In the Tank Destroyer illustration is a Tank Destroyer patch with no eyes applied. A 2nd Marine Division error type is also illustrated. Its shape does not even resemble the authorized design. Error types have a higher value and are similar to coins and stamps in that regard.

46th Division patches. Left: Correct design. Right: Error type with reversed colors

Distinctive insignia (DIs)
Top: Left to right: 4th Cavalry Regiment, 47th Division, 38th Division, Bottom: 1st Army, 4th Army, and 81st Division. DIs may have clutch- backs, pin-backs, or screw-backs.

2nd Marine Division - Left: Correct design. Right: Error type

Felt - Refers to the material, normally used as the background of a patch. Felt is a wool base with a fuzzy feel and is very soft to the touch. Felt was extremely common on insignia from pre-Civil War to Korea.

French made - Some insignia were produced for American forces in France. The most common are embroi-

Just a sample of the thousands of U.S. distinctive insignia

dered on twill and fully embroidered patches, and metal and enameled distinctive insignia.

Gabardine - Coarse cloth

German made - Germany became a source of private-purchase patches primarily during the period of occupation after the war. Primary construction types include bevo, embroidered and bullion. The addition of bullion trim to existing American embroidered patches was also common. Some metal insignias were also produced in Germany. Patches discribed as having a basket weave, open weave or fruit weave are usually German-made.

Green back: Refers to the color of thread covering the back of a patch ("snow"). The predominant color of snow is white, but green, black, and other colors can be found. Despite many dealers advertising patches with green backs as being a scarce variation, green backs are common and there should be no disparity in price whether a patch has white or green thread on the back. *Most* green back patches will have olive drab borders. The sahde of green may vary from forest green, to a very brownish olive drab.

34th Infantry Division. The 2nd and 34th appear brown, but are an olive drab when examined closely.

Group - Normally means an assortment of items associated with the same person. A "medal group" normally means a bar(s) or collection of medals, devices, etc. that were awarded to the same recipient. Groups, when named and/or numbered, often make further research possible and can afford some certainty of provenance. Groups are also more reflective of the recipient's overall service and experiences. Groups consequently command a higher price than separate, unattributed, but otherwise identical medals and decorations. Groups of insignia that are additionally accompanied by paperwork and award documents are even more desirable and valuable.

Example of a "group" of items

This group is attributed to Henry W. Berquist. It includes documents, collar brass, dog tags, patches, DI, pins, and wings from his wartime service. Henry participated in the Navy's V-5 flying cadet program, and later served as a gunner on B-17s in India. This is a fascinating and varied group of mementos that have been kept in the cigar box named to him. The cigar box originated from India and cost two Rupees in 1945. Theater made patches like those shown in this group cost GIs about as much as the cigars.

Herringbone - Refers to a type of cross-stitch, twill weave which looks like slanted parallel lines. Herringbone shirts and pants appear as though they have columns of vertically stacked "V's" side by side. Combat fatigues worn by the army and marines were frequently made from herringbone material.

Examples of green back patches

The green back examples are on the left, the more common white back types are on the right. *From top to bottom:* 2nd Infantry Division, 44th Infantry Division,

Distinctive herringbone pattern from a USMC shirt.

HMed / HM'd - Hallmarked. This means a maker name or distinctive marking appears on the insignia. Some pieces may have four or five different markings on the reverse.

Examples of medal insignia bearing hallmarles

Integral tab - Patches like the 10th Mountain Division, and various airborne divisions included tabs as part of their design. Most frequently these tabs are manufactured separately and are sewn above the patch. Some tabs however, are manufactured as part of the patch. In other words, the patch and tab are one piece. This is referred to as being an integral or "attached" tab design. *See "Attached Tab" above.*

Italian made - Several patches and other insignia were produced in Italy. Primary construction types include bullion on felt or wool, silk/bevo, hand-embroidered, and the addition of bullion trim to American embroidered designs. Some metal insignia were also produced.

Khaki - Refers to the material color of uniforms and the background or edge color of insignia. Although often inappropriately used, "khaki" normally means a light tan shade. Officially known as "Army Shade No 1".

Leather - Many insignia during WWII were manufactured from leather. These are most frequently aviation related designs made for wear on leather flight jackets. The most common types are painted designs on a leather background or multiple pieces of leather which were painted and then sewn together to achieve the desired design. An example would be the Ledo Road patch that is frequently found in a seven piece-leather design. Other types are silk-screened, or decals applied to leather. Leather was very prevalent in Europe, but less so in the pacific because leather tended to decompose in the moist, tropical environments.

Above: A leather 10th Army Air Force patch manufactured in the China Burma India Theater during WWII. This piece is comprised of eight individual pieces of leather. The yellow, white, red, and blue are painted. This patch was never used and is in mint condition.

Lot - An assortment of items. Multiple pieces that are offered together.

Merrowed - Merrowed edges on insignia became the norm during the last years of the Vietnam War. Many WWII patches have a raised edge that is often, wrongfully, thought to be merrowed. Close examination will allow the collector to tell the difference. Most cloth patches from the 40's and 50's have a raised edge where a heavy thread border was applied to prevent fraying. Merrowed edges normally have a higher, more pronounced ridge with a ribbed appearance. A very prominent locking stitch, that has the appearance of a small chain, can be found around the inside of this ridge. The reverse, or back side of the merrowed edge will resemble a tire track design. Merrowed patches usually have a tail of locking stitch (like an umbilical chord) attached. This tail may be glued or taped down. Patches with merrowed edges, other than one variation of the 506th Parachute Infantry Regiment patch, were manufactured between about 1964 and the present. Many reproduction WWII patches have merrowed edges and can easily be detected as fakes. High quality reproductions have a cut edge, like the originals and are harder to distinguish.

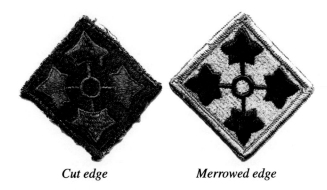

Cut edge   Merrowed edge

Close-up of 4th Division patches. Cut edge *left and* merrowed edge *right*

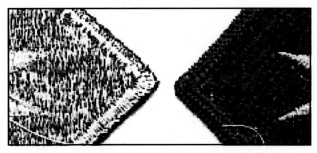

40th Division patches (reverse sides). Cut edge *left and* merrowed edge *right*

Close-up of pigtail on a merrowed 40th Division patch

Mothing - Refers to damage caused by moths over a period of time. Some materials are more susceptible to moths such as wool and felt. The extent of damage should be described in detail. Moth damage will reduce the worth of most patches in proportion to their degree of scarcity. Common patches are essentially worthless with moth damage. Patches that are fairly difficult to find may be worth half of their premium value when found with moderate moth damage. Ultra rare patches may retain most of their value even when damaged by moths because they are so difficult to find in any condition.

Named / #d or Numbered - Indicates that the piece bears an assigned number, or the name of the recipient. The name/number may be engraved or stamped. Numbers frequently are located on the edge of medals. In the case of certain medals / decorations this can indicate the period it was issued and can facilitate the identification of the recipient and acquisition of the recipient's service records. A named and/or numbered piece is more valuable and desirable than an otherwise identical unnumbered piece.

Air Medal named to Cpl. Robert A. Dalton, Detachment 101, OSS, Burma

Olive Drab or "OD" - Normally refers to the background color or edge color of a patch. Olive drab is the color of army uniforms until 1957. Therefore, genuine insignia found with the olive drab trim is likely pre-1957 vintage. Olive drab is a greenish-brown shade. Officially known as "Olive Drab Shade No 33 or 51".

Overseas made - Major military ports and facilities around the world are usually surrounded by tailor shops. Installations that have been established for long periods of time and have large military populations sustain local businesses that manufacture renditions of authorized insignias. Some of these shops use sophisticated and modern machinery and the insignia they produce are almost identical to American factory produced items. Other, less sophisticated operations, produce a variety of insignia that vary in quality from fair to extremely crude. Often times errors in spelling or details occur creating some interesting variations. Some are completely handmade and are literally one of a kind. Japan, Okinawa, the Philippines, Korea and Germany are areas that have seen a prolonged presence of American forces. Thousands of private purchase, overseas made uniforms and insignia originate in these countries. There is a distinction between theater made and overseas made patches. "Theater made" refers to patches produced in a particular area during wartime operations or occupation. Theater made pieces usually have a substantially higher value than U.S. made standard types. "Overseas made" simply implies that the patch was made someplace other than the U.S., but does not suggest wartime manufacture. Hundreds of patches are produced overseas every day. Overseas types are generally not considered to be much more desirable than U.S. made items. The collector should seek clarification when these terms are used because they are occasionally used incorrectly. **Note** - Many collectors have an interest in insignia that were made in Vietnam during our involvement there. Vietnamese made items are commanding very high prices on today's market. These collectors need to be aware that patches made in the previously mentioned countries are frequently, erroneously represented as "Vietnamese made" and are sold to unsuspecting collectors for substantial sums of money.

Patina - A thin crust of discoloration normally found on copper, brass, and bronze. This usually appears as a green substance. It is normally associated with some age, and occurs as part of the natural oxidation process. "Patina" is also used to indicate age-related discoloration to other materials.

PB - Pin-back. Also an indicator of older vintage to include WWII. Pin-back designs normally have a pin which is hinged on one end and is secured on the opposite end by a rolling latch or hook.

Pronged back - May be thin wire or wide metal prongs. Difficult to approximate the age by this type of device. Prongs have been used from the 1700's to current. Many nations including Canada, England and Australia use prong devices on their badges and insignia.

Repo, repro, or reproduction - These are terms used to indicate recent copies of period designs. See "collector copy" above.

Reverse - Refers to what would be considered the back side of an item. Normally used when describing medals, badges and other items that have details on both sides.

SB - Screw-back. This is normally a feature or indicator of earlier manufacture 1800's - 1940's. This design uses a threaded post which is pushed through a hole in the clothing. It is then secured by a threaded cap screwed onto the post. Some types of insignia such as larger cap badges are still made in a screw-back design.

Screw-back insignia

Separate tab - When tabs are found that are not factory affixed to their respective patch, they are referred to as being "separate". An example would be a airborne tab which accompanies, but is not affixed to, an airborne division patch.

9th Airborne Division patch with separate tab

Silk - Refers to the base material or type of thread used to manufacture a patch. Silk was used in many early American embroidered patches. Primarily associated with Asian, particularly Chinese and Japanese manufacture.

Pin-back insignia

Sizing: This refers to a opaque/clear glazing substance that is applied to the reverse side of a patch. The primary purpose of sizing was to make cloth patches rigid. Experiments were conducted where adhesive was added to the glaze. When heated (ironed or pressed) the adhesive became tacky and held the patch to clothing so they could be sewn more easily. Additionally, liberal applications of the glaze to cut-edges helped to inhibit fraying. Quite often, the glaze is not too conspicuous and requires close scrutiny to detect. It will usually appear as sparkles on the edges and back. On some patches I have noted that only traces of the substance are still visible it looks like tiny bits of glass glittering. The application of sizing on patches is a characteristic of post-war manufacture. Although sizing is believed to have been introduced, to a limited extent, around 1946, it was not widely used until the 1950's. Sizing is found on many high-quality reproductions which otherwise look authentic. This is an important characteristic to be aware of. In some cases, it is the only feature that will identify a patch as post-war.

Snow - This was a predominant feature of embroidered patches manufactured in the 1930's and 1940's. Rather than waste colored thread, once at the back, the machines would draw from the white bobbin. This white on the reverse is commonly referred to as "snow" because it almost appears as if you are looking at the patch through a blizzard of white thread. Even when the back of WWII patches are not covered with snow, the high points on the reverse edges will be largely white. As cotton thread, rayon and silk were replaced in later years by comparatively inexpensive nylons and other synthetic materials, this became unnecessary. The simplification and automation of the manufacturing process also made constant bobbin changing unnecessary. Most patches manufactured in latter years have a conspicuous absence of snow on the reverse. The only difference between the front and reverse sides is that the front looks more finished. In other words, the reverse of a new patch is like a slightly out of focus camera. The colors and designs are easily distinguishable and essentially intact. The front will appear the same, but with a crisper, cleaner, more focused appearance. Conversely, it may be impossible to determine what the front of a WWII vintage patch looks like by studying the reverse side. Occasionally, some WWII or earlier manufacturers used other colors for the reverse. These are normally colors that were used in many designs and were consequently purchased in the greatest quantities. For example, olive drab was used in many designs and was also used by some manufacturers as a border color for their patches. Consequently, several manufacturers used olive drab on the reverse. Snow can be found in other colors like black and blue, but this is relatively uncommon. Interestingly, the snow color may not be used in the design on the front of the patch. Snow, in and of itself, is not an absolute technique for determining good from bad. But it is reliable to such an extent that I will rarely purchase a WWII, fully embroidered patch if there is not a significant presence of snow.

Front sides of a 6th Airborne Division (phantom) patch and 22nd Division (phantom) patch. It is difficult to tell which is original and which is a reproduction.

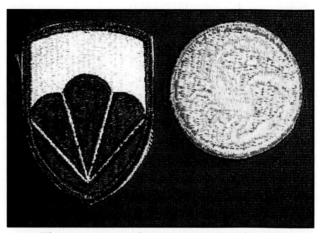

The same two patches in reverse. Note how the reproduction 6th has almost no snow on the reverse. The 22nd is covered with snow. This is the most fundamental method of detecting fakes.

Two USMC 51st Defense Battalion patches. Again, it is difficult to tell which is original and which is a reproduction.

*The same two patches in reverse. The snow covered
original is immediately obvious on the left.*

Left: *Another example using two USMC 18th Defense
Battalion patches. Both look fairly good from the front.*

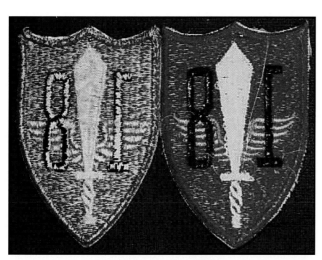

The original is on the left.

Sterling - This normally indicates that the piece
is marked "sterling". Contrary to the maddening belief of many antique dealers, the sterling silver con-

tent of a marked piece does not represent any significant value. It is important only because it indicates an
older piece. Manufacturers began using other processes with less silver content to reduce costs, largely
after WWII.

Studley - George W. Studley was a manufacturer
of patches during WWII. Unlike the Patch King,
Studley concentrated his efforts on *only* those units
that wore patches during WWI. Studley produced miniature variations of these patches as well. In fact, most
of the small patches referred to by dealers as variations for wear on the overseas cap are actually Studley
products for WWI veterans. Many patches offered for
sale today, and advertised as being from the 1920's
and 30's are Studley patches produced during the
1940's. They are usually executed on discs of wool or
felt. Studley produced small catalogs featuring his
patches, medals, badges and other items during the
war. Although patches are frequently identified as being "Studley" types, it is almost impossible to determine if a patch was produced by Studley, the Patch
King, or other more obscure outlets.

Subdued - This refers to the Vietnam to current
practice of manufacturing cloth insignia in green and
black for utility and camouflage purposes. In most
cases a patch that is done with primarily green and
black are subdued versions and can be considered
newer types. Exceptions include the 1st Army, 81st
and 89th Divisions, and numerous WWI designs. The
Air Force often incorporates blue, red, green, brown,
yellow and other colors in their current subdued designs.

Subdued patches

An assortment of subdued patches. Subdued colors became the norm for battle and utility uniforms
during the Vietnam War. But some patches like the 1st
Army and 81st, and 89th Divisions were made in subdued colors during WWI and WWII.

Theater made - Means that the particular piece
was manufactured in a foreign country during wartime
or immediate post-war occupation..

T-pin - Self explanatory. An indicator of older manufacture (WWII or earlier).

Twill - Refers to the material type, normally used as the background of a patch. Twill normally has parallel diagonal lines or a "ribbed" appearance.

Ultraviolet (UV) - Refers to one method of detecting reproduction/current patches. Patches from WWII utilize cotton or silk threads. White silk or cotton do not react to UV light. Many newer patches use synthetic threads. Synthetic white thread will glow brilliantly when exposed to UV. Any patch that does react to UV light is not WWII vintage. No exceptions. Do not confuse cheap "blacklight" bulbs with UV light. "Blacklight" bulbs will not work for this. See "Blacklight".

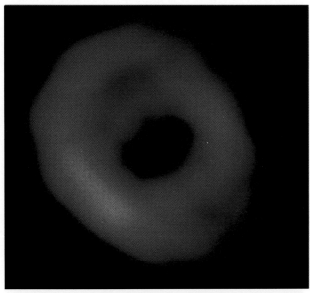

Ultraviolet light reaction

Above: The ghostly glow in this illustration is the white nylon thread, in a reproduction 9th Airborne Division patch, reacting to ultraviolet light. There is an original patch, with white cotton thread, beside it to the right, which does not react at all. Any patch that reacts to UV light, in part, or in whole, was manufactured after WWII.

Uncut - Cloth insignia was normally mass produced. The designs were executed repeatedly along strips of material. These strips were then cut into many individual patches. On occasion, a collector will find a strip of patches that were not individually separated. Also, particularly with cloth rank insignia, branch insignia and wings, when cut individually or in pairs, there was still an excess of the backing which needed to be trimmed before the patch was sewn on. Patches with this excess material still intact will be described as uncut.

Uncut embroidered colonel's insignia

These embroidered colonel's insignia were made for the collar. This pair has never been separated and trimmed in preparation for wear. This is a clear example of how standard, factory embroidered patches were manufactured during WWII. Designs were repetitiously sewn onto strips of fabric. They then had to be cut into individual squares, with one design per square. Finally, any excess fabric was cut from around the design and the design was ready to be sewn on a uniform. Note that in the case of collar insignia where a matched pair is required, every other design must be facing the alternate direction.

Unauthorized - Refers to any insignia that was never formally approved by military authority. Many common patches were never authorized. Most of these were sanctioned for "local wear" only, meaning they could only be worn while assigned to a particular unit, in a particular region. Designs worn by the Desert Air Force, Merrill's Marauders, Panama Hellgate, Kiska Task Force and Women's Auxiliary Ferrying Squadron are just a few examples of the many patches that were never officially recognized but were extensively used. Many unauthorized patches were designed by members of the unit. Patch designs are known to have been variously proposed by the commander, a member with some artistic ability, or perhaps as the result of a contest within the unit. Often times it worked like this: Once the design was accepted, everyone chipped in a few dollars. If a soldier wanted one, he paid for two. If he wanted two, he paid for three, and so on. This gave the unit an immediate surplus to issue to new members as they arrived. Many units had a fund that all members made a token monthly contribution to. This fund would eventually pay the cost of future patch orders. Unofficial patch designs number in the thousands.

Unissued - Refers to an insignia that is authentic and of its respective period, but was never worn and shows very little or no wear whatsoever (mint condition). I prefer worn and used examples of insignia. Those who would strive to collect pristine examples will probably be seeking unissued types. When dealing with a reputable dealer this is not too risky. Other than reputable dealers, one needs to be wary of old insignia represented as being unissued. Remember, even unissued patches that have been around for 50+ years will often exhibit some indications of age. Unissued is actually a misnomer. "Unused" is more appropriate.

Variation - Refers to any insignia that strays in some aspect from the design approved by military authority. This can include size, shape, material, color and detail omissions or additions. Other examples of variation include patches with and without the olive drab border, or different color "snow" on the back, or even thread patterns that vary from manufacturer to manufacturer. Many of the insignia designs of the 1940's originated during WWI. Because of less rigid criteria regarding the design and wear of shoulder insignia during that war, thousands of variations existed. Many were hand-made and are literally one of a kind. Several have a basic design but added colors represent the branch of service or designate a particular sub-unit. An example would be the 2nd Division. The Indian head and star would be applied to a background of various shapes and colors. The shape and color of the background identified the soldier's specialty and specific unit within the division. Marine units attached to the division were easily identified as were artillerymen, machine gunners, engineers and so on. During WWII, to simplify the process considerably and reduce cost, units authorized to wear a shoulder patch were required to keep the design relatively simple and were to use one combination of colors. In spite of this, variations exist which include color codes for sub-divisional units. One example is the 89th Division patch. This design can be found with color inserts in the lower center of the "W". The First Army is another common example and can be found with various colors in the top and bottom of the "A". Other variations known to exist were manufacturer errors and can include reversed colors and reversed (backward facing) designs. Variations provide an interesting facet and depth to any collection. **Note:** Military regulations state that any patch design featuring a head or face, will be made with the design facing to the wearer's forward (dexter) or full face (affronte') when worn. The tradition of wearing a "combat patch" on the right sleeve has prompted the creation of variations with the head or character facing the opposite direction so that the design would face forward when worn on the right sleeve. Variations are illustrated throughout this book.

Wax-back – Refers to patches having an opaque film covering the reverse side. Besides serving as a stiffening agent, the substance also becomes tacky when heated and works as an adhesive to help keep the patch firmly affixed to a shirt or jacket. The film looks like a thin layer of plastic or wax and is very obvious. This is a characteristic of very recently manufactured patches.

Worsted wool - Smooth, hard-twisted thread. The material has a smooth, hard surface and is used as a background. It is the result of a combing process.

Degrees of availability and scarcity: Some items were made by the millions while others may be literally one of a kind. Some pieces were frail and perishable, while others were hardy and solid. Some items were rigidly accounted for and others were "procured" by the thousands as souvenirs. These are all examples of factors that determine the availability of items to collectors, and to a large degree, their value on the market. Obviously, rare items will be priced higher than common items. The terms most often used do describe availability of a particular piece are:

One of a kind An unusually superior example of it's respective type. Highly unusual, or with significant historic association. So rare that it may literally be the only example known to exist. This term is often used to describe museum quality pieces.

Ultra rare
Very rare
Rare
Very scarce
Scarce
Common (No reference to scarcity usually implies that the item is common).

Dealers use these codes somewhat subjectively. The items are often coded based, at least to some extent, by the respective dealer's personal experience and expertise.

THE INTERNET &
SURVIVAL AT THE AUCTION

I am surprised constantly by the number of collectors and dealers who express serious reservations about using the internet for the purpose of buying and selling their wares. Most of these fears can be dispelled with nothing more than a little familiarity with how internet auctions are organized and administered. The common perception seems to be that you are essentially entrusting money or material to anonymous, untraceable individuals. A virtual black-hole if you will. As a Chief of Police, I am as sensitive to, and wary of, opportunities for fraud and theft as anyone is. I shared these reservations before experimenting with the internet. What I have discovered is that internet auctions are governed by a number of security mechanisms and checks and balances to protect users. The potential for fraud and theft exists as it does anywhere. But users that invest a minimal amount of time familiarizing themselves with the security and payment options are perfectly safe at the auction. Common sense is really the only advantage one needs to successfully negotiate the internet. I have dedicated this section to readers who are pondering the possibility of trying the internet as a buying/selling option. It is intended to be a fundamental introduction to the process. In three years of continuous activity, both buying and selling, I have had only one unresolved issue with a disreputable vendor. In that case, the person's questionable reliability was readily available to me and I failed to check it. I am not always satisfied with my purchases, but the auction allows you to deal with vendors who offer refunds and exchanges. Most importantly, I have developed a hundred friendships with people who share my interest, which I would otherwise have never come into contact with.

The internet has created the ability to locate wanted items without difficulty. When I first began hunting for patches on the internet, I was dumbfounded. Patches that had eluded me for decades, I found in hours.

Everyone with internet access literally enjoys a "24-7" military show in the comfort of their home. No travel, no incidental expenses, no crowds, and no distractions. The consequence of the convenience however, is competing with collectors worldwide for any given item. Collectors and dealers from every corner of the globe, from every experience level, and from every economic stratum are competing for every patch. Like real auctions, undisciplined buyers can find themselves preoccupied with the competitive nature of the auction and lose sight of judgment and common sense. Some people become intoxicated by the ability to overcome all others with the stroke of a key. Not infrequently, when ego displaces judgment, buyers find themselves paying enormously exaggerated sums for something that is simply not that valuable. As long as buyers continue this behavior, those disproportionate prices will represent the fair market value. I have seen patches that you would have been delighted to sell for a

$1.00 two years ago, bringing $30.00 at auction. I have seen patches that sold for $125.00 two years ago, selling for $600.00-$700.00 at auction. From a long-time collector / investment perspective this is rewarding in a sense. But if you are a new collector or if you want to continue an existing collection these prices are, at the very least, discouraging.

Another interesting phenomena of the auction is its sensitivity to incidental influences. A vivid example was the immediate demand for the Ranger patch and 29th Infantry Division patch after the movie *Saving Private Ryan* hit the screens. Overnight, the selling prices for these two patches had climbed 800% in some instances.

The internet has been the single most successful collecting tool I have ever used, but I bid responsibly. I remind myself regularly to be objective when buying. Do I *really* need this patch? Do I *really* want this patch? What else could I buy with the bid I am about to make? If I wanted to sell this later, could I find someone else to offer this much? Can I find this later for less? If I pass on this one, will I ever find another?

Ask yourself these things throughout the auction process. Assess and reassess. Don't let your ego operate the keyboard.

Familiarize yourself with the auction you decide to use. Spend time consulting the rules, procedures and services available. There are also sections providing helpful tips to new sellers and buyers. These tips are the result of experience. Many of these tips are the result of complaints and subsequent investigations. The auction houses are very interested in minimizing problems and they have gone to some effort to provide their customers with the information necessary to recognize potential pit-falls. Tips on how to describe and market your items are also provided.

SELLING:

When selling items, marketing is everything. Items that are not accompanied by photos are simply unattractive to most buyers. The photos and description will dictate what sort of interest is generated in your item. When photos are not provided, shoppers will usually move on, rather than depend upon the seller's credibility and knowledge. Many auctions offer free photo listing services. This is normally restricted to a couple photos and if more are desired you have to pay a fee. I rarely offer items for sale other than patches. Two scans, one of the front, and one of the back, allows potential buyers to assess a patch thoroughly. It requires a substantial amount of memory to store and transmit images. Consequently, there are restrictions on the size of the image files accepted by the auctions. Be sensitive to this and adjust the size or quality accordingly to meet the auction's specifications.

To search for an item, a potential buyer types in key-words describing the type of item they are interested in and then click on the "search" button. So, as a seller, your item description (title) must include words that are likely to be used by customers looking for items like yours. If you have a rare WWII Ranger patch variation, you want to title it as such. "Rare WWII Ranger patch variation". This title will appear as a search result to anyone that searched using the words "rare patch", "WWII patch", "Ranger patch" and so

on. Remember that you have an opportunity to reach a lot of interest groups with your title. If you title this item WWII patch, you will reach customers with a general interest that review anything under the "WWII patch" title. However, if you title it as I suggested above, you will reach generalist collectors who search under "WWII patch", collectors who look under "rare patch", and collectors who specialize in Ranger memorabilia and search under "Ranger patch". Additionally, you have reached collectors who are specifically interested in variations and may search under something like "patch variation". In short, a well thought out title will contain key-words that are likely to be used by multiple groups of collectors and thus increase the number of viewers and competition for your items. Experience has shown me that specialist collectors are frequently more advanced in their hobby. They tend to be more willing to pay premium prices for good material. When appropriate, key-words that are used by specialists like "rare", "variation" and so on are essential.

Pricing is the other most important issue for sellers. You need to monitor the auctions constantly and keep abreast of current price trends. Your patches will need to be priced accordingly. Pricing items too low can generate suspicion of their authenticity. Good images will alleviate these concerns. Pricing items too high will discourage potential buyers. It is interesting to note that patches tend to sell themselves. Even when listed with a very reasonable minimum bid, buyers will compete until a fair market price is reached. There are thousands of collectors at the auction who are experienced and recognize good material. I have seen patches start a dollar and sell for hundreds. Even when a seller does not recognize the value of a patch, the buyers will. They will compete with one another until it reaches its reasonable worth. Sometimes the prices are driven by collectors who, for whatever reason, crave a particular item, and will pay far in excess of its market value to own it. Setting your minimum bid too low is less of a concern than setting it too high.

Pricing is also a method that buyers can use to verify your level of expertise. If you list a patch for fifty dollars that commonly sells for ten, you are making a statement that you are not familiar with your material. This statement will erode the customer's confidence in your ability to properly judge the age, condition and authenticity of your material as well.

The seller can choose the payment options that he/she will accept. There are a number of escrow services and innovative payment plans available to protect the buyer and the seller. The options are plentiful enough to ensure that everyone can find a comfortable arrangement.

Buyers can rate sellers based upon the speed of delivery, the quality of communications between the seller and buyer, the quality of the item(s), the responsiveness to inquiries, and the accuracy with which the item was represented. These ratings are visible to everyone at the auction. If you conduct yourself in a courteous, efficient, timely manner, your ratings will be great. If you fail to answer questions, if you fail to respond promptly at the close of an auction, if your item is not as described, if your delivery of the item is slow, or if you exhibit other poor business practices, your ratings will effectively insure that nobody does business with you. Occasionally, glitches occur. I have had trouble making contact with buyers and sellers because of errors in email addresses. I have had items seriously delayed in the mail and on one occasion, lost completely. I make it a practice to accept responsibility for any glitches whether they are my fault or not. Whether it is a refund or a replacement item, it pays huge dividends to treat your customers well. In each case where an item failed to arrive in a reasonable time and a refund or exchange occurred, the item did eventually arrive. Every customer has acknowledged that and returned the money or one of the items they received. There is also a number of mailing options that allow you to trace the item you sent. This will help to prevent circumstances like an unscrupulous buyer receiving your item, but claiming that it never arrived. Most of my customers are repeat customers and I have yet to receive anything other than excellent ratings. There is no such thing as too much of an investment in your reputation and credibility.

Above all else, describe your material precisely. I tend to be overly critical when describing my items. This way, if the buyer is satisfied with the object from the description,

they will be delighted when they receive it. This practice will also result in favorable feedback. I have found that there are buyers for everything regardless of condition. But details like moth nips, tears, stains, and so on are extremely important to many collectors. It is your responsibility to provide a description that allows the buyer to know precisely what they are bidding on.

Another tip that will bring you favorable consideration is rating your buyers. Anytime a transaction occurs, the buyer and seller have an opportunity to rate each other. Most buyers are prompt with payment and courteous to deal with. Rate them accordingly. The goal at the auction is to secure as many positive feedback comments as possible. Having a substantial history of successful business interactions ensures that even the most discerning people will gladly conduct business with you. Assisting your customers in developing their reputation through positive feedback from you, when they earn it, encourages future loyalty to you as a vendor.

BUYING:

As a buyer, you are interested in the reliability and reputation of your suppliers. Every vendor (and every buyer) will have a number accompanying their auction name. This number represents the number of times this person has received feedback from people he/she has bought from and sold to. By clicking on this number, each feedback comment can be reviewed. There is also normally a summary, which breaks the feedback into positive and negative categories. At a glance, you can determine how much business this individual does at the auction, and how satisfied or dissatisfied his/her customers are. Inadvertent glitches and disputes will occur in any business environment. But, if a vendor has 500 transactions recorded and only 1 negative experience is listed, they are probably a good person to do business with. I have seen vendors and buyers with several thousand favorable feedback entries and not one negative comment. Obviously, these are great people to do business with.

Avoid doing business with anybody who has any pattern at all of negative feedback. Also, if a vendor has 1000 positive comments and 1 negative, you can check the nature of the negative entry. Many times it is apparent that this was a particularly "difficult" person, who would not have been happy regardless of how the transaction went. Fortunately, people like that are seldom encountered and do not surface with any regularity. My rule of thumb for selecting vendors is a minimum of 25 feedback entries with no negative comments. I may overlook negative comments on a ratio of 250 positives for every negative. This may be a bit unreasonable, but there are countless vendors with hundreds of positive comments and no negatives whatsoever. You need to determine your own comfort zone through time and experience. The beauty of this system is you can be as selective and cautious as you wish.

Sellers will normally list their payment preferences and return/exchange policies. If it is not listed, inquire prior to buying. This alleviates hassles later should you be dissatisfied with your item. Reputable dealers will always offer an inspection period and return option. If a seller refuses to accept a return, don't do business with them. It's as simple as that.

If you are concerned about sending money to a stranger regardless of their feedback history, utilize one of the many escrow programs available. These are easy to use and provide another layer of protection for both parties. Whatever method you select, forward your payment promptly. The other party will usually mirror your ethic. Quick payment will secure very positive feedback from sellers.

As I explained in the "SELLING" section, the item search process utilizes key-words to locate, select and display items that match the subject of your inquiry. If you type in the word "patch" and then hit "search", everything on the auction with "patch" in the title will appear for you to review. This may literally contain thousands of items. Some examples of what may appear include: police patch, iron on patch, inner tube patch repair kit, Cabbage patch dolls, patch-work quilt, etc. As you can see, it may be a substantial benefit to narrow your search. If you type "WWII patch" and hit "search"a you will narrow your search to any item with "WWII patch" in the title. However, what some people do not consider is that vendors may not use your precise wording to title their items. Therefore, the buyer should attempt a number of searches using variations of the key-words. I routinely search for items using the following word combinations:

WW II patch(es)
Shoulder sleeve insignia
AAF patch(es)
USMC patch(es)
WW2 patch(es)
Rare patch(es)
Army patc (es)
Navy patch(es)
Shoulder patch(es)
Army Air Force patch(es)
Marine patch(es)
U.S. patch(es)
World War Two patch(es)

and numerous combinations of these and other key-words. Some vendors do not specialize in military goods, but may list random items as they acquire them. Consequently, they don't know the proper name of the item and use less descriptive titles. I have found numerous desirable patches while searching with more obscure key-words like:

Old patch(es)
Military patch(es)
Unknown patch(es)
Unidentified patch(es)

Use your imagination and experiment with key-words. This will help you eliminate having to review unnecessary items, will increase the number of desired items you locate, and will allow you to search under titles that many other collectors don't use, thus minimizing your potential competition. If you are a highly specialized collector, you can save time by entering key-words that narrow your searches to very specific items. For instance:

Eighth Air Force patch(es)
China Burma India patch(cs)
509thAirborne patch(es)
8th Air Force patch(es)
CBI patch(es)
509th AB patch(es)
The possibilities are almost infinite.

CHANGE OF IDENTITY CAUTION:

Most auctions require a lengthy membership application, which usually involves obtaining your credit card number, name, address, and so on. Having these records serves as good incentive for people to behave acceptably. With your membership acceptance, comes an auction ID. This is your "handle" and this is what buyers and sellers at the auction will know you by. There are some legitimate reasons for changing this identity later. But there are also circumstances where a change may be desired because of a history of negative feedback comments. Most auctions will place a symbol next to the auction ID of anyone who has changed their auction ID. eBay uses a small sunglasses symbol. This simply means that the person in question has changed their auction identity for some reason. Further inquiry can be made to determine if this was the result of bad business practices. Make sure you are familiar with the symbol that your auction has dedicated for this purpose.

Something that buyers will learn very quickly, is that many buyers will "snipe" an item at the very last second. They will avoid participating in any bid activity to create the illusion that there is no interest in the particular item, which gives the current high bidder a false sense of security. At precisely the last moment before the item closes, they will submit a bid leaving you with no opportunity to counter-bid. This can be a frustrating ordeal. I have walked away as the high bidder, many, many times, confident that nobody else is interested only to check after closing and finding that someone outbid me in the last few seconds. The logic is this: Let's say an item goes up for auction for seven days. The minimum bid (the least amount the seller will take) is $10.00. I bid $11.00 the first day. A competitor bids $12.00. We continue this exchange for seven days. It is clear to see that the price will escalate quickly. If we each bid only $1.00 each day, the price will have reached $22.00 by closing time. But, let's say I bid $11.00 the first day. My competitor ignores the item until the very last moment of the very last day, and then bids $12.00. My competitor wins and saves himself six days worth of escalating bids ($10.00)..

Another problem is a buyer's inability to monitor the bid activity night and day. I, for instance, can only bid in the evenings and on the weekends. Items close twenty-four hours a day. I can't monitor an item "24-7" in case I need to make a counter-bid. Therefore, the auctions have developed automatic bidding.

Automatic bidding allows you to type in the maximum amount you are willing to bid on an item. As people bid against you, your bid amount will automatically increase incrementally. If the item exceeds your maximum bid amount, you will simply cease to be a participant. The increments are listed and they are proportionate to the cost of the item. An inexpensive piece may go up in increments of .50. A more expensive item may go up in increments of $5.00. As an example let's say an item goes up for auction and the minimum bid is $5.50. I am willing to pay a maximum of $10.00. The bid increment is listed as .50. I enter my maximum bid amount of $10.00. My bid amount will be displayed as $5.50 (the minimum bid). Then someone bids against me ($6.00). My account will automatically up my bid to $6.50. My competitor will receive a message saying that he/she has been outbid. This will continue until a competitor bids in excess of $10.00 (my pre-determined maximum), at which time I will cease to be a participant and the person submitting the $10.50 bid will receive a message that he/she is now the current high bidder. If nobody bids against my initial bid of $5.50, I will win the item at that price.

My personal technique is to determine my absolute maximum and then submit it. I will then walk away. If I win, I win. If I lose, I lose. But I have found that if you monitor the progress closely, your ego will assume control of the keyboard and you will continue to submit "just one more bid". If you can't live without a particular item, submit a maximum bid that is the absolute most you can live with spending. I have entered conservative maximums on patches I desperately wanted, and then lost. I have then regretted not submitting a higher maximum bid to begin with because I would gladly have paid more to have it. Determine your absolute maximum, submit it and walk away. This will alleviate regrets. If it goes for more, you are satisfied because you simply could not afford it. If you win, you will not be sick because you overspent.

CONCLUSION:

In three-four years of using the internet, I have advanced my collection more than the preceding decades combined. It is a wonderful tool and I highly recommend it to everyone. Just apply good judgment, adhere to the rules, and educate yourself prior to beginning. Happy hunting!

* To get you started, the following are excellent sources of authentic military insignia. You can email them to find out where they have items listed, or can converse with them about your want list and interests:

Panama Dave – db@dc.infi.net
Vintage Productions – vinproduct@mindspring.com
The Patch People – ragpic1@aol.com
Wartime Collectables – wartime@camden.net
The author can be contacted at – dcbrown@mcsi.net

BIBLIOGRAPHY

Smith, Richard W. & Roy A. Pelz; *Shoulder Sleeve Insignia of The U.S. Armed Forces 1941-1945,* Richard W. Smith, Henersonville, TN; 1981.

Britton, Jack & George Washington JR.; *Military Shoulder Patches of The United States Armed Forces.* M.C.N. Press, Tulsa, OK; 1990.

Stein, Barry Jason; *U.S. Army Patches An Illustrated Encyclopedia of Cloth Unit Insignia*;University of South Carolina press, Columbia, South Carolina; 1997.

Grosvenor, Gilbert. *Insignia and Decorations of The United States Armed Forces*; National Geographic Society, Washington DC; 1945.

LIFE Magazine; Oldsmobile ad. 1944.

LIFE Magazine; August, 1945.

Author unknown. *The Story of The 390th Bombardment Group (H).* "Privately published"; 1947.

Lind, Ragnar G., Capt. USAF, editor. *The Falcon, History of The 79th Fighter Group, USAAF, 1942-1945*; F. Bruckmann, Munich, Germany; 1946.

King, Elizabeth W. *Heroes of Wartime Science and Mercy.* National Geographic Society; Washington DC; December, 1943.

Stanton, Shelby L. *Order of Battle, U.S. Army World War II*; Galahad Books, New York. (1991).

Paulsen, Valdemar. *U.S. Army Facts and Insignia*; Rand McNally & Company; 1918.

Newsweek Magazine. *A Pocket Reference Guide For Army, Navy, Marine Corps Insignia*; Readers Digest supplement; March, 1943.

Rosignoli, Guido. *Army Badges and Insignia of World War 2*; The Macmillan Company, New York; 1972.

Kerrigan, Evans E. *American Badges and Insignia.* The Viking Press, New York; 1967.

The Manions. *The Manions Military Auction House, Military Antiques Auction*

Catalog 104; Kansas City, Kansas; 1987.

The Manions. *The Manions Military Auction House, Military Antiques Auction Catalog 106*; Kansas City, Kansas; 1988.

Morgan J. L. Pete & Ted A. Thurman. *American Military Patch Guide*; MOA Press; Fountain Inn, South Carolina; 1997.

The *Trading Post,* produced by the *American Society of Military Insignia Collectors (ASMIC).* Undoubtedly the best on-going resource for collectors of American insignia.

George B. Harris III, *Military and Historical Americana*; catalogs- 1980s-1990s; Alfred, New York.

ABOUT THE AUTHOR

    Chris Brown is a native of upstate New York. He took an interest in military insignia at the age of eight. In 1978, Chris began his career in law enforcement, in New York. He moved to Oregon in 1985. His assignments have included: patrol, drug enforcement, supervisor of a multi-agency drug enforcement team, patrol supervisor, SWAT officer and commander, patrol division commander, and he is currently the Chief of Police in Roseburg, Oregon. Chris is an instructor of myriad law enforcement subjects, and has instructed for federal, state and local agencies. He is also involved in providing law enforcement instruction at colleges and the Oregon Police Academy. Chris holds a BA in organizational management, and he is a graduate of numerous professional schools including the Oregon Executive Development Institute and Northwestern University's School of Police Staff and Command. Chris has written published works on drug enforcement and leadership. He lives with his wife Donna, and has three children: Tiffany, R.J. and Kelsey.

INDEX